This book revea...
the apostle...

Grandpa,
Teach Me To Pray

Jesus commanded. "When ye pray, say..."

Dr. James Wilkins

Printed by Calvary Publishing
A Ministry of Parker Memorial Baptist Church
1902 East Cavanaugh Road, Lansing, MI 48910.
www.CalvaryPublishing.org

All Scriptures are taken from the King James Bible.
ISBN # 978-0-9802043-4-6

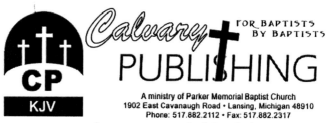

Calvary
PUBLISHING
FOR BAPTISTS
BY BAPTISTS
CP
KJV
A ministry of Parker Memorial Baptist Church
1902 East Cavanaugh Road • Lansing, Michigan 48910
Phone: 517.882.2112 • Fax: 517.882.2317
www.calvarypublishing.org

ALAN PATRICK CAPPS
Husband, father, High school math teacher and youth worker

REBECCA WILSON
Wife, schoolteacher and youth worker

DANIEL CAPPS
Faithful church member and youth worker

OLIVIA WILKINS
Schoolteacher, faithful church member and soul-winner

SARAH FLORES
Wife, faithful church member and medical doctor

LYNDOL JAMES WILKINS III
Faithful church member and college student

LOREN WILKINS
Faithful church member, soon to be college student

JEANE BOWMER
Wife, surgical nurse and youth worker

KOREY FINCH
Young minister and faithful church member

KLAY FINCH
Dedicated to becoming a youth pastor

KYLER FINCH
Student and faithful church member

MAY EACH OF THEM HAVE A RICH MILLENNIUM

WAYS OF USING THIS BOOK

If I were asked, which is the best way that *Grandpa, Teach Me to Pray* could be used I would answer;

☐ **FOR PERSONAL PLEASURE**
If one would read this book it would prove educational as well as pleasurable.

☐ **FOR TRAINING CHILDREN**
The student edition is divided into a five day study for a student to do one section each for the five week days. Parents are admonished to "bring up a child in the way that he should go". Reading and discussing each days activity on a daily basis would be a prosperous way to obey this command.

☐ **FOR DAILY DEVOTIONS**
If one made it part of his personal devotional time it would produce great spiritual growth and confidence in the person, and motivate him to become a more dedicated disciple of Christ.

☐ **FOR DISCIPLING CONVERTS**

The biblical way of developing a new convert into being "a worker" instead of being "a sitter", is by placing a faithful role model over him for the first few months of his spiritual life. New converts, as well as small children, learn more from observation than from what they hear. So they need personal role models to train them properly.

☐　　　**FOR HOME BIBLE STUDY**
There is such a weakness in the area of prayer in the lives of most people, that many would gravitate to a home bible study ON PRAYER. There is nothing that a person could do to help people more than teach them "how to pray." Get five people together for a home bible class, and we will furnish the teacher with his own autographed copy FREE!

☐　　　**FOR SUNDAY SCHOOL CLASS**

☒　　　**ALL OF THE ABOVE WOULD BE THE AUTHORS ANSWER!**

Foreword

One of the strategies of the enemy in the times of war where water is very scarce, is to poison the "**water holes**".

This is exactly what the devil has done to the foundational doctrines of the Bible. He has poisoned each of God's holy doctrines by contaminating its precious truth with a mixture of lies.

The devil has poisoned the minds of many Christian about God's command "**to be filled with the Spirit**" (Ephesians 5:18) by the confusion of speaking in tongues and the misuse of Spiritual Gifts.

There is no doctrine that the devil has worked harder **to blind the minds of God's people** than in the area of prayer.

The model prayer, wrongfully referred to as "The Lord's Prayer, is the most powerful weapon available to a Christian. The devil has successfully blinded the minds of God's children to its potential by the vain, empty repetition of multitudes of religious people. This boring repetition of **these precious words has blinded the minds** to the absolute command of Jesus to follow the model prayer in establishing a healthy prayer life. Jesus' exact words to the Apostles were, **"when ye pray, say**." He then gave them a model in which they were to follow every day.

The model prayer is not a simple little formal prayer of empty words but **it is God's tool of motivating** his disciples into a powerful army of workers who can not be defeated.

In the Great Awakening of 1734 John Wesley and George Whitfield **taught their disciples to pray the model prayer every day.** The results of that great revival changed America and England back into godly, Christian nations. You will find the same principles in *Grandpa, Teach Me To Pray.*

Grandpa, Teach Me To Pray comes in two formats – a spiral bound workbook form as well as in conventional book form. The symbol (+) indicates a sentence where an answer to a test question can be found.

Bulk Prices are available.

Table of Contents

LESSON #1
GRANDPA, TEACH ME TO PRAY 12

LESSON #2
OUR FATHER WHICH ART IN HEAVEN 27

LESSON #3
HOLLOWED BE THY NAME ALMIGHTY
GOD IS THE BELIEVER'S FATHER 41

LESSON #4
THY KINGDOM COME 56

LESSON #5
THY WILL DONE IN EARTH AS IT IS
IN HEAVEN 74

LESSON #6
GIVE US THIS DAY OUR
DAILY BREAD 90

LESSON #7
FORGIVE US OUR DEBTS AS WE
FORGIVE OUR DEBTORS 107

LESSON #8
LEAD US NOT INTO TEMPTATION,
BUT DELIVER US FROM EVIL 126

LESSON #9
FOR THINE IS THE KINGDOM 141

LESSON #10
THINE IS... THE POWER 163

LESSON #11
THINE IS...THE GLORY 183

LESSON #12
FOREVER   207

LESSON #13
AMEN   222

Lesson One

And it came to pass, that, as he was praying in a certain place, when he ceased, one of his disciples said unto him, LORD, TEACH US TO PRAY, as John also taught his disciples. And he said unto them, WHEN YE PRAY, SAY, Our Father which art in heaven, Hallowed be thy name. Thy kingdom come. Thy will be done, as in heaven, so in earth Give us day by day our daily bread. And forgive us our sins; for we also forgive every one that is indebted to us. And lead us not into temptation; but deliver us from evil. Luke 11:1-4

Additional Scripture Reference:
Matthew 6:6-15
Luke 5:5-13

LESSON ONE
GRANDPA, TEACH ME TO PRAY

A BOY BEGAN THE PROCESS OF LEARNING TO PRAY. (+)

INTRODUCTION: A young man with a desire to grow as a Christian, approaches His Godly grandfather for help and counseling. The simple question, "GRANDPA, TEACH ME TO PRAY" begins a series of thirteen lessons which transform the young man's life and helps him find his purpose as a Christian. This series will strengthen and change your life.

GRANDPA, I'VE GOT A PROBLEM.

Timothy, age 17, had a troubled look on his face as he walked the final steps up the stairs where his grandpa was sitting.

Grandpa glanced down and noticed the serious look on his grandson's face, and began a little song that he and his grandson had sung so often together, "**Smile a while and give your face a rest**" and instantly Tim's serious look melted into a bright, smiling, face and he said, "Grandpa, I knew I could count on you."

"How's that?" came grandpa's cheerful reply.

Tim responded, "Well, I've got a problem and I thought you would understand and…and…

"Help you with it." grandpa finished the sentence.

"Yeah, it's kind of embarrassing."

"Embarrassing, you say?"

"Yeah, although I know I am a Christian...you remember when I got saved, don't you, Grandpa?"

"Sure do, Timothy, it is vivid in my mind, just as though it happened yesterday."

Tim nodded, "me too and it was seven years ago, and grandpa, I'm still praying like I did when I was a baby…"(+)

Grandpa waited as Tim continued on. "I'm still praying like mama first taught me."

As Tim dropped his head his grandfather kept silent in order for Tim to express his problems.

"Grandpa, some times I almost pray, "now I lay me down to sleep… and I know that is kid stuff and I need to grow up. I still say, bless mama and daddy and grandma and grandpa…"

Grandpa put his arms around his grandson's shoulder and said, "You never want to stop praying that prayer son. But you want me to help you to learn to pray. Is that the problem Timmy boy?"

LONG VERSION OR SHORT VERSION

Tim lifted his head and said, "That's the problem. Will you teach me how to pray Grandpa?"

Grandpa laughed as Tim lifted his head.

"Do you want the long version or the short version?" came Grandpa's question.

"Grandpa, I'm almost a man now. I will be 18 on my next birthday. I'm serious about God's work, and I want you to help me learn how to get my prayers answered. (+) I know that if I ever do what the Bible commands, 'To be strong in the Lord,' I am going to have to learn to pray." (+)

"Long version, HUH?"

"Whatever it takes, Grandpa - whatever it takes."

"Let me start the process of teaching you how to pray by asking you a couple of question's, okay? began Grandpa.

> Men may spurn our appeals, reject our message, oppose our arguments, despise our persons- but they are helpless against our prayers.
>
> -Sidlow Baxter

"Okay, Grandpa, but you will find out that I'm not very smart on Bible things."

PEOPLE HAVE ALWAYS HAD YOUR PROBLEM

"Tim, many years ago when I was a young Christian, I learned that the problem of praying was a common problem."

DISCOVERED THAT SOME DIDN'T PRAY IN PUBLIC

I noticed that the pastor would call on the same men to lead in public prayer in the church services. (+) He may have eight or ten different men, but it was generally the same eight or ten. One day I asked a friend who had been a member of that church, "Why does the pastor always call on the same men to pray? Why doesn't he call on Brother Jones to pray?"

"Oh, Bro. Jones doesn't pray in public," was the answer.

DISCOVERED AN ADDITIONAL PROBLEM

As I became more advanced as a pastor, I discovered that those who did not pray out loud in the church services generally did not pray at home either. (+) It was a common thing for some friend or member of the family to tell me, the new pastor, that so and so does not pray in public.

What do these have in common?
"Ye must be born again"
"WHEN YE PRAY, SAY"
"Pray without ceasing"

They are all commandments of God!

DISCOVERED THAT MOST PASTORS OFFERED
THE WRONG SOLUTION.

There were enough men in the churches that did not know "how" to pray, and refused to lead in public prayer that many pastors were now having to address the problem.

"Their solution, Tim, was to preach more sermons on the subject of prayer. (+) They would teach on topics such as;
> **Prayer**
> **The need of Prayer**
> **The great prayers of the Bible**
> **The hindrance to getting prayers answered**

"But the preaching on why we ought to pray **did little to solve the problem.**" (+)

DISCOVERED A SIMPLE WAY OF
SOLVING THE PROBLEM.

"The simple method that I learned which helped people to begin praying more, was to teach people "HOW" to pray.

I would create a simple prayer list and then show them;

> How to begin – *Dear Heavenly Father*
> What to pray for – *a prayer list*
> How to finish their prayer – *In Jesus' Name.*

In order to get them to pray out loud, I would remind them that Jesus said that one should go to the prayer closet and shut the door. (+)

I askd them why? Why shut the door? My answer was, one shuts the door in order to pray out loud. He hears his voice as he begins his prayer of, "Dear Heavenly Father," and as he prays down his prayer list.

One may ask, "Why is it important for him to hear his voice as he prays?"

The answer of why he should pray out loud is two fold -
First - Prayer is a means of ministering as well as communion with God. (+) We are to learn to pray for others. By praying out loud we learn how we can teach others to pray.

Second - The second reason is the solution to the problem, and enables more people to have confidence in praying out loud in a public prayer.
- They know how to begin.
- They know how to pray for needs.
- They know how to finish their prayer and they have heard the sound of their voice and are no longer inhibited in praying in public.

"I see that Grandpa," Tim responded, "and that's great!"

"Wait a minute young man." That was my poor human way of solving part of the problem."

DISCOVERED GOD'S WAY

God had already been asked by his disciples for help in learning to pray.

Whereas, the method I taught was helpful in getting people to pray more, and better prayer: God's way of teaching people how to pray, transforms them from struggling Christians to conquering Christians. (+)

> **Prayer is the most important thing in my life. If I should neglect prayer for a single day, I should lose a great deal of the fire of faith.**
>
> **-Martin Luther**

THE DIFFERENCE BETWEEN THE MODEL PRAYER AND THE LORD'S PRAYER

"Let me ask you this question, Tim, what is the difference between the **Lord' s Prayer, and the Model Prayer?**"(+)

"The Lord's Prayer and the what?" came Tim's reply.

"The model prayer," repeated Grandpa.

"I've never heard of the model prayer, but I sure know the Lord's Prayer," came Tim's cheerful response. And with that he started quoting, "Our father, which art in heaven...."

Grandpa allowed his grandson to finish quoting all the verses and then commented, "Well done, Tim, I'm proud of you. Now, which did you say that was, the Lord's Prayer or the model Prayer?"

"The Lord's Prayer, Grandpa, everyone knows that," came Tim's positive response.

Grandpa said, "Son, I'm sorry to have to tell you that your bright and **positive answer is wrong**."

The smile was replaced with a look of shock, "Wrong," Tim said. But grandpa, I've heard those verses taught as the Lord's Prayer all of my life." (+)

"I know, Son, but that is man's interpretation and not the Bible's." (+)

"Well, if it is not the Lord's Prayer, then, what is it grandpa?" And as he finishes his question it seemed to dawn on him, and he joined his grandfather in saying. "IT IS THE MODEL PRAYER, isn't it?"

"The prayer you quoted is in reality the model prayer that the Lord gave to his disciples," instructed grandpa.

THE APOSTLES ASK JESUS YOUR QUESTION

"Tim, the apostles asked Jesus the exact question you asked me?"

Tim looked a little confused and asked, "What was that grandpa?"

Grandfather continued, "What question do you think the apostles asked Jesus, Tim?"

"To Preach, the apostles were all preachers, weren't they?" responded Tim.

"Yes, Tim, they were but we do not have one instance where any of the apostles ever ask Jesus to teach them how to preach."

"To Soul-win?" was Tim's next question.

"They may have asked him to teach them how to win souls, but we do not have that request recorded. There are several accounts where Jesus taught people to win souls, but there is no place where they ask him to teach them how."

"No, Timmy boy, the question the apostles asked Jesus is the question you asked me," grandpa continued. "The apostles never ask him to teach them how to preach or how to win souls, but they did ask HIM TO TEACH THEM TO PRAY."

"Really, Grandpa? Did the apostles ask Jesus to teach them how to pray? Where is that in the Bible, I want to show my friend Fred?"

"Look right here in the gospel of Luke 11:1. One of his disciples said unto him, LORD, TEACH US TO PRAY AS JOHN ALSO TAUGHT HIS DISCIPLES." (+)

Tim repeated, "Teach us to pray as John..."

Grandpa interrupted, "John the Baptist!"

Tim continued, "....also taught his disciples. Wow! Grandpa, I don't feel so dumb now. If the apostles ask Jesus to teach them to pray; then, it is okay for me to ask you to teach me how to pray."

THE LORD'S PRAYER

"If Luke 11:2 is the model prayer, Grandpa, then where do you find the Lord's prayer in the Bible?"

"Tim, the Lord's Prayer is properly referred to as the Lord's prayer, because it is the prayer that Jesus prayed to his father in the garden of Gethsemane, the night before his crucifixion."(+)

In the gospel of Luke 11:1 One of his disciples said unto him, LORD, TEACH US TO PRAY AS JOHN ALSO TAUGHT HIS DISCIPLES

"Is it a complete prayer that Jesus prayed to his father, Grandpa?"

"Yes, Timmy, it is a whole prayer that Jesus prayed to his father; and do you know that in that prayer he prayed for you?"

"For me?"

"Yes, he prayed for you, and for me also."

"Where in the Bible is that prayer, Grandpa? I want to read it."

"The prayer began in the Gospel of John chapter 17 and continues throughout the whole chapter."

"Let me ask you another question, Tim."

WHY DON'T WE FOLLOW THE MODEL PRAYER TODAY?

"Tim, you remember when you and I used to put together your model airplane?"

"Sure, Grandpa, I still have a couple of them on display in my room. But why do you ask that question, Grandpa?"

"Do you remember what a hard time we had on that last plane?" continued Grandpa.

"Yes, we must have read those plans a dozen times before we figured out how all those pieces went together." (+)

> The Lord's Prayer is properly referred to as the Lord's prayer, because it is the prayer that Jesus prayed to his father in the garden of Gethsemane, the night before his crucifixion

"But, when we finally read the instructions and followed the plans to make the model – it was simple. Right?" (+)

"Right, Grandpa, but what does all that have to do with teaching me how to pray?"

" The apostles asked Jesus to teach them to pray, and Jesus GAVE THEM A MODEL TO FOLLOW WHEN THEY PRAYED."(+)

"Just like the airplane had instructions, Jesus gave the apostles instructions, or A MODEL TO FOLLOW WHEN PRAYING." (+)

"Oh, said Tim, I see now why they call it the Lord's Prayer... I mean, THE MODEL PRAYER. Now, Grandpa, if it is a model for us to follow, then why don't we hear that taught, and why don't we follow it? (+)

But, Grandpa, I've got to go now… but, I'll be back tomorrow and continue our lesson on prayer."

HOMEWORK ASSIGNMENT

"Great," responded Grandpa. "but remember, we are working on the long version. Look at Luke 11:2 for a minute before you leave. Read it for me. Just until I tell you to stop."

Tim begins to read, "And he (Jesus) said unto them, **when you pray, say**…"

"STOP," commanded grandpa. "Tim, doesn't that statement, 'when you pray, say..' sound like a command to you?" (+)

"Before you leave, I have a home work assignment for you tonight."

"Homework? Grandpa? Homework?" "Yes, **first** I want you to tell me how fast light travels. **Second**, how far it is to our sun, and **thirdly** look up information on the sun and the star, Antares." (+)

"Okay, Grandpa. I'll see you tomorrow." Tim replied, "and thanks a lot Grandpa… You are the greatest, but I don't see what the homework assignment has to do with me learning how to pray."

"Trust your old grandpa," he said as he waved goodbye. "You will." Go over Jesus' statement, **'when you pray, Say** . . .' a couple of times, and tell me what you think he meant. See you tomorrow."

"It sure doesn't sound like a suggestion, Grandpa. But I really have to be going . . . .Good-bye" waved Tim as he walked down the steps.

POINTS TO PONDER

❖ **Are you living a life where your children would come to you for Spiritual help? (+)**

❖ **Are you setting a spiritual example for your children to safely follow? (+)**

❖ **Is your prayer life your strength or weakness, in your walk with God? (+)**

❖ **Study the following lessons on prayer, and it will enrich as well as change your life.**

❖ **Does the statement Jesus made to the apostles, "WHEN YOU PRAY, SAY..." SOUND LIKE A SUGGESTION OR A COMMAND?**

Lesson Two

Be not ye therefore like unto them: for your Father knoweth what things ye have need of, before ye ask him. After this manner therefore pray ye: OUR FATHER WHICH ART IN HEAVEN, Hallowed be thy name. Thy kingdom come. Thy will be done in earth, as it is in heaven. Give us this day our daily bread. And forgive us our debts, as we forgive our debtors. And lead us not into temptation, but deliver us from evil: For thine is the kingdom, and the power, and the glory, for ever. Amen.
Matthew 6:8-13

Additional Scripture Reference:
Matthew 6:6-15
Luke 5:5-13

LESSON TWO
OUR FATHER WHICH ART IN HEAVEN

HOMEWORK COMPLETED

"Hello, Timmy boy, what have you got there?" was grandpa's opening salutation as his grandson entered the door.

"It's my homework, Grandpa. It caused quite a stir at my house. You got everyone in our family wondering about you. I ask a simple question about prayer and you give me homework that has nothing to do with prayer. At least our family couldn't figure it out if it does."

"Come on into my study and let's see what you have," said Grandpa, as he led the way into his favorite room.

Tim sat down next to grandpa, who asked, "What did you learn Timmy boy?"

"I LEARNED THAT THIS IS A BIG, BIG WORLD. In fact, this universe is so huge that scientists had to use a special unit of measurement in order to express how gigantic the universe is." (+)

Tim turns to his notes and continues his explanation. "The astronomer's yard stick is a light year: the distance light travels in one year is calculated by the second." (+)

"By the second, you say, interjects Grandpa, that was one of the questions in your homework assignment, wasn't it?"

"You know it was, grandpa, and the answer is that **light travels at the rate of 186,273 miles per second.**" (+)

> **The spectacle of a nation praying is more awe-inspiring than the explosion of an atomic bomb. The Force of prayer is greater than any possible combination of man-controlled powers, because prayer is man's greatest means of trapping the infinite resources of God.**
>
> -J Edgar Hoover

"Per second," echoes Grandpa as he feigns amazement, "light travels 186,273 miles per second which means that light would travel about 6 trillion miles in a year. At 186,273 per second, light would circle the earth at the equator **seven and half times a second.**" (+)

"You also wanted me to look up how far it was to our sun," Tim said, as he looked up from his paper.

With pride in his voice he boldly stated, "**About 93 million miles.** Using the measurement of how fast light travels when one beam of light leaves the sun's surface, it would arrive at the earth eight minutes later." (+)

"Very good," beamed Grandpa.

THE VASTNESS OF THE CREATION OF GOD

"That's unbelievable Grandpa, but the rest of the stuff really blew my mind."

"And what is that Tim, that really blew your mind?"

"The vastness of **Antares** and Hercules and the whole universe," came Tim's answer.

"As big as our sun is … it would take, as he glanced to his paper, **sixty four million of our suns to make one star the size of Antares!**" Tim exclaimed. (+)

"Sixty-four million of our Suns," mused grandpa."

"But Grandpa, it would take **one hundred million stars, the size of Antares to make one star as gigantic as the star Hercules.** Grandpa, did you know that in our galaxy… and there are many galaxies, that the milky way is 100,000 light years in diameter? (+) And it is traveling…"

"Traveling, you say?"

"Yes, the whole universe is traveling. It is revolving at about 200 miles an hour, and will take two million years to complete one revolution on its axis. (+) And Grandpa, did you know that our planet, earth, is traveling too?" "But, according to our scientists, it is going **three directions at the same time.**"

Tim seemed to run out of breath as he shared his discovery.

"It travels! Our earth's traveling three directions at the same time, you say," came Grandpa's comment. (!)

"Yeah, but when mom and I looked that up; I didn't understand how that could be possible, but that fact has been proven by our modern labs, computers, and scientists."

"What is the possibility of some of these stars or suns running together and bringing destruction to our planet, Tim?"

"According to our scientists there is absolutely no chance of that happening, Grandpa. Every planet, every star, in every galaxy is in its…"as he looked back to his paper.

"Orb," said Grandpa.

"Yes that's the word they used, orb, and Grandpa they say that our galaxy and earth only loses one, one hundredth of a second every one hundred years." (+)

"But Grandpa, what does all this stuff, the sun, how fast light travels and the hugeness of Antares HAVE TO DO WITH PRAYER?

THE VAST UNIVERSE REVEALS A POWERFUL CREATOR

"Tim, before answering your question, please answer a few more questions for me."

"Okay Grandpa, what is it?"

"Where did this vast universe come from? Who is the one who keeps all these massive bodies in their places or orbs?" (+)

"Again Grandpa, that's easy," Tim answered. "IT IS GOD."

"God must be a very big or powerful God to create and then maintain all those vast spaces with their huge galaxies which revolve through the heavens, and yet stay in their assigned places. (+) Don't you think?

"Yes, Grandpa, but what's that got to do with prayer? My time here is almost over today and I still don't know how to pray."

"Well, Timmy boy, let's see what you have learned about prayer so far."

"What is the difference between the Lord's prayer and the Model prayer?"

> **What do these have in common?**
>
> "Honor thy father and mother"
> "Open wide thy mouth"
> "WHEN YE PRAY SAY"
>
> **They are all commandments of God!**

"You showed me yesterday that the Lord's prayer was the prayer Jesus prayed in the Garden of Gethsemane. And Grandpa, I did read in John 17 where Jesus prayed for me." (+)

"Good Boy."

"The Model prayer is where Jesus answered one of his disciples request to teach them to pray."

"and…" asked Grandpa?"

"and, what Grandpa?"

"What did Jesus do when his disciples asked him to teach them to pray?" (+)

"Did he give them a lecture on why they should pray more, or did he ignore their request all together?" (+)

"Grandpa, he didn't do either. Jesus gave them **a model prayer to follow** when they prayed."

"Really?"

"Really, Grandpa, We read that model Prayer yesterday."

"How did Jesus instruct the apostles to start their Model Prayer, Timmy?"

THE CREATOR AND CONTROLLER IS OUR HEAVENLY FATHER

"Why, everyone knows that. He taught them to begin by addressing God as their heavenly father."

"Tim, think about what you are saying. They are to address the powerful God who keeps all the vast galaxies in their proper orbs as,

> **The big, powerful God in heaven is my spiritual father, and since I am one of His born again kids, he wants to hear and answer my prayers.**

'FATHER'." (+)

"The powerful God who created this awesome universe, and keeps everything working so smoothly is the One we are to pray to and address as **OUR HEAVENLY FATHER.**"

Tim sat there for several seconds and then said, "Grandpa, I now understand what all that science stuff you had me look up has to do with prayer. Jesus gave the apostles a Model Prayer to follow when they prayed, and the first principle they were to recognize was that they were praying **to a big God that was able to answer big prayers.**" (+)

"That's good, Timmy boy, but you only got part of the lesson. Who are the people in your life that love you the most, that you turn to for help when you have a need or a problem?"

"Why you, and mom, and dad," Tim answered.

"Yes, Tim, everyone knows that you can get almost anything you want from your mother." (+)

"Oh Grandpa, that's not really true. When mom says no, it is pretty hard to change her. But again, Grandpa I don't see what that has to do with learning to pray." "The point is, Tim, that the big God of heaven is **your Spiritual Father** who loves you far more than your mom and dad love you. He wants you to learn to get things from Him, just as you have learned to influence your mother."

"Wow Grandpa, what a lesson! The big, powerful God in heaven is **my spiritual father,** and since I am one of His born again kids, he wants to hear and answer my prayers." (+)

"That's great Timmy, but I have two more thoughts I want you to consider before our lesson for today is over."

"Remember our annual trips to the loft in the big barn the last six or seven years?"

"Why yes, Grandpa, but Sarah (Tim's younger sister) and I have gone up there many other times when you were busy."

"Yes, I know. But what was the attraction? What caused you to look out of that knot hole in the loft wall?"
"To see the mother bird feed her babies, you know that?"

"Yes and what was the thing that caused you the most wonderment in watching the mother feed her babies?"

"I still can't believe **how wide the baby birds would open their mouths**. Their mouths seemed to be double jointed." (+)

OPEN WIDE THY MOUTH

"Look at this scripture here in Psalms Timmy, and read it out loud."

Tim began to read, "I am the Lord thy God which brought you out to the land of Egypt: open wide thy mouth, and I will fill it." (Psalm 81:10) Tim sat there for a minute thinking as grandpa waited. Then

Tim continued as if he was talking to himself. "God wants us to open wide our mouth and ask Big prayers so he can . . . . ."

"**Answer our prayers,**" continued grandpa. (+) "Just like the old mother bird loves to feed her babies, God loves for us to pray big prayers so he can answer our prayers . . . fill our mouths, so to speak. Also Tim, God uses the example of birds to illustrate how he desires to hear our prayers and take care of us. But in doing so he asks, "Are you not more important than they (the birds)?" Matthew 6:26 (+) He is really saying, I take care of the birds but Tim, YOU ARE MY BOY! And I will really hear your prayers and take care of you."

"Wow, Grandpa, that's awesome!" Exclaimed Tim. "What was the other verse, Grandpa?"

"Jeremiah 33:5," repeated Grandpa.

Tim read, "Call unto me, and I will answer thee, and shew thee **great and mighty things** which thou knoweth not." (Jeremiah 33:5)

"Tim, in this verse God is encouraging his people to ask **Big Prayers.** He tells them that he wants to show them, 'great and mighty things,' in answer to their prayers." (+)

REMEMBER, THE BLANK CHECK

"Tim, do you remember the

> "I am the Lord thy God which brought you out to the land of Egypt: OPEN WIDE THY MOUTH, AND I WILL FILL IT." (Psalm 81:10)

35

blank check your father gave you last Christmas?"

"Do I? It scared me to death to think that he would trust me with a blank check."

"What was the occasion, Tim?"

"Dad promised to take me and let me pick out the motor bike of my choice, but at the last minute he was called into work. So he called Mr. Carter at the bicycle shop and told him I was coming in and to cash the check."

"Do you know, Timmy boy, that God has given some people a blank check against the bank of heaven, and has already authorized God to cash it? Naturally, all prayers are conditional, which means there are certain conditions which must be met before the blank check can be cashed." (+)

"Where is that promise, Grandpa?"

"Right here in the gospel of John. Read it for us."

"John 15:16 – Ye have not chosen me, but I have chosen you, and ordained you, that ye should go and bring forth fruit, and that your fruit should remain: THAT WHATSOEVER YE SHALL ASK of the Father in my name, he may give it you."

WHATSOEVER (BLANK CHECK) YOU ASK OF MY FATHER

"Now, Tim, remember the first great point in learning to pray and in following God's model. Who is the most powerful being in the universe?"

"God, who is **our Heavenly Father**," answered Tim.

> **"Call unto me, and I will answer thee, and shew thee great and mighty things which thou knoweth not."**
> **Jeremiah 33:5**

"He is your spiritual father by birth. He commands us to open our mouth wide (big prayers) because it his good pleasure to bless us. He wants to show us great and mighty things..." emphasized Grandpa. (+)

"What a lesson, Grandpa, what a lesson! I'm sure going to work hard in order to learn how to pray properly."

"I want to give you a verse to work on Tim."

"Another homework assignment?" laughed Tim.

"Yes, memorize Ephesians 3:20, and come for lesson number three tomorrow." "*Now, unto him that is able to do **exceedingly abundantly above all that we ask or think,**_according to the power that worketh in us.*" quoted Grandpa as he ended the lesson. (+)

"Wait a minute Grandpa." Tim exclaimed. "Aren't you forgetting part of my homework assignment?"

Grandpa thought for a second, "Oh, yes, replied Grandpa, and what did you conclude?"

"When Jesus answered the apostles request to teach them how to pray he said, 'WHEN YE PRAY, SAY . ..' I talked to mom about that statement and we both thought that Jesus gave the apostles a model to follow while praying and **commanded them to follow it**. (+) But that raised another question Grandpa."

"What's that, son?"

"Does that command, 'WHEN YOU PRAY, SAY...' apply to us who are alive today?"

"Good question! Continue to study on that point and we will see you tomorrow."

POINTS TO PONDER

❖ **My Sovereign Father KNOWS all things.**

❖ **My Sovereign Father CONTROLS all things.**

❖ **My Sovereign Father WANTS ME TO RULE AND REIGN with his Son during the Millennium.**

❖ **My Sovereign Father wants TO HIRE ME to work in the final harvest of 6 ½ billion souls.**

❖ **My Sovereign Father OFFERS ME FAVORITE STATUS for 1,000 years if I do his work in my life NOW.**

Lesson Three

And it came to pass, that, as he was praying in a certain place, when he ceased, one of his disciples said unto him, LORD, TEACH US TO PRAY, as John also taught his disciples. And he said unto them, When ye pray, say, Our Father which art in heaven, HALLOWED BE THY NAME. Thy kingdom come. Thy will be done, as in heaven, so in earth Give us day by day our daily bread. And forgive us our sins; for we also forgive every one that is indebted to us. And lead us not into temptation; but deliver us from evil. Luke 11:1-4

ADDITIONAL SCRIPTURE REFERENCE:
Matthew 6:6-15
Luke 5:5-13

LESSON THREE

HOLLOWED BE THY NAME ALMIGHTY GOD IS THE BELIEVER'S FATHER

"Hello, Timmy boy, who's your little friend?"

"Oh, Grandpa," answered Sarah, Tim's younger sister. "Tim came home so enthused and excited about what he learned that I decided that he wasn't going to have all the fun. And besides, I learned the memory verse before he did." And with that she repeated Ephesians 3:20, only when she got to the word him, she inserted (**my heavenly father**).

"Now unto **my heavenly father** that is able to do exceedingly abundantly above all that we ask or think, according to the power that worketh in us." (+)

Grandpa applauded her effort and said, "Welcome, the more the merrier."

Tim burst into the conversation by saying, "Grandpa, when we began to read the model prayer, we started a verse or two above where the model prayer began, and you know what?"

"What?" Grandpa answered.

"From the beginning of chapter 6 verse one, through the eighteen verses, Jesus referred to God as "Father" TEN TIMES." (+)

"And..," Sarah interrupted her brother, "he would always put a personal pronoun in front of Father, 'Thy Father' or 'Your Father.' Which means that Jesus really wants us to view or picture the Almighty God of heaven, not as some far off distant God who is busy running the universe, but he wants us to approach him as our father who loves us."

"Kids," Grandpa interrupted, "let me add a little fuel to your excitement; Sarah, I see that you have your Bible with you. Turn to Romans 8:15 and read it."

"For we have not received the Spirit of bondage again to fear," read Sarah, "but we have received the Spirit of adoption, whereby we cry, Abba, Father."

Both young peoples eyes were focused on their Grandfather's face, waiting for his explanation. He began by saying, "This verse teaches the Spirit of prayer. Notice, whereby we cry, Abba, which is the dearest term for father. Abba

God Only

Lord, in the strength of grace,
With a glad heart and free,
Myself, my residue of days, I
consecrate to Thee

Thy ransomed servant, I
Restore to Thee Thine own;
And from this moment live or
die to serve my God alone
-Chas. Wesley

is not the formal term, Father, but the endearing term "Daddy." (+) It is used like a little child looking up into her father's face and pleading, 'daddy please'."
"Grandpa, that's great." commented Tim.

"No, that is awesome, to think that God, our father really wants us to come to him in prayer, injected Sarah. And he wants us to begin our prayer by remembering that we are talking to our daddy." (+)

FATHER IS USED ONE HUNDRED FORTY-SIX TIMES

"Kids, since we are discussing coming to God in prayer as our father; may I ask you to use your computer."

"Use our computer, Grandpa?" came Tim's surprised inquiry.

"Why," asked Sarah?

"Get your Bible program that your mom and dad uses to check scriptural facts, and to compare Scriptures."

"And do what," asked Sarah a little impatiently?

"Check on how many times a derivative of the word 'Father' is used by Jesus."

"Remember that in the Gospel of John, Jesus is referred to as the Word." (+)

> Abba is not the formal term, Father, **but the endearing term "Daddy."** It is used like a little child looking up into her father's face and pleading, **daddy please**

"In the beginning was the Word, and the word was with God and the Word was God. The same was in the beginning with God. All things were made by him, and without him was not anything made that was made. John 1:1-3," quoted Sarah.

"Grandpa, I never understood why they called Jesus, The Word," said Tim.

"Words are used to express the thoughts and feelings of a person. Jesus was called the Word because he came to express the love and nature of God through his teaching and life. (+) He came to show the world what God was like through his daily life and teaching."

"But back to my question," said Grandpa. "How many times do you think Jesus referred to or called God his Father?"

"Twenty," came Sarah's guess.

"More than that," answered Grandpa.

"Fifty," said Tim.

"Double that number," Grandpa said.

"One-hundred?" replied Sarah.

"I still want you to look it up for yourself but in order to illustrate and emphasize God as your Father, I will tell you now. Jesus referred to God as his Father either directly or indirectly, a **total of one hundred forty-six times in the Gospel of John**. (+) The reason I want you to look it up yourself, is to see that this figure is accurate and to see the different ways and times that Jesus referred to God as His Father."

"No doubt he was emphasizing what he taught the apostles in **the model prayer,** in order to get that fact into their minds. They would think of God as their Father, instead of thinking of him JUST as God." (+)

"Another reason, no doubt, God is seeking fellowship with his children, and is attempting to get them to look up to him, and rely on him as children rely upon their dad." (+)

"One hundred forty-six times, that is almost unbelievable," commented Tim in wonderment.

"Jesus is really working to get His point across, and teach us to learn and accept that God is our Father," remarked Sarah. (+)

COME BOLDLY TO THE THRONE OF GRACE

"Tim, you were going to say something your mother taught you, "reminded Grandpa.

"Oh yes, mom pointed out a Scripture that states that God wants us to come boldly unto the throne of grace...," stated Timmy.(+)

> **What do these have in common?**
> "WHEN YE PRAY SAY"
> "Thou shalt not take the name of the Lord in vain"
> "Let every thing that hath breath praise the Lord"
> **They are all commandments of God!**

"The throne of grace is where God hears our prayers," explained grandpa to Sarah who had a puzzled look on her face. "In fact, the rest of the verse explains why we are to come to the throne of grace-that

45

we may attain help in time of need. (Hebrews 4:16) Our father wants to hear from us and help us." (+)

HELP IN TIME OF NEED

"Sarah," said Grandpa, "I'm sorry, but what does it mean? **We may attain help in time of need?**"

"It probably means that God is always there to help – in every situation and problem," offered Tim. "I read a scripture where Jesus said that men ought always to pray and faint not."

Sarah answered, "I believe that God answers prayer, but that statement sounds like God somehow or another helps people especially when they are praying. Is that right?"

"That's exactly right, Sarah. Sometimes a Christian just doesn't know which way God wants him to go, or he gets into a trial and is really hurting. He doesn't know what, or who to believe. It is here that God, your Father, gives someone to help you in time of need." (+)

"Someone like you, Grandpa? I know you really have helped me --- many times," said Tim.

"God may use me or your parents or someone else, like your pastor or a friend, to help you. But God offers greater help than humans can give."

"Really Grandpa, who?" asked Sarah.
"**The Holy Spirit**," answered Grandpa. "You see, no human can see the innermost thoughts of a

person. They cannot see the hurt or the fear or pain a person may be experiencing; but God can."

"Many times we don't know what to pray for, or we don't have the words to express our inner feelings. But your Heavenly Father sees your thoughts, your indecision, yes, and even your confusion, and he dispatches someone to help." (+)

"I don't doubt what you are saying because I believe it," commented Tim. "But is there a clear scripture which states that?"

"Good boy, Tim," congratulated Grandpa. "Always turn to the Bible for the foundation of truth or doctrine. Sarah, turn to Rom. 8:26-27."

Sarah read, *"Likewise the Spirit also helpeth our infirmities: for we know not what we should pray for as we ought: but the Spirit itself maketh intercession for us with groanings which cannot be uttered. And he that searcheth the hearts knoweth what is the mind of the Spirit, because he maketh intercession for the saints according to the will of God."*

After Sarah finished reading, Tim stated, "Wow! Grandpa. Everything you stated is right there in those two verses."

"Helpeth our infirmities," quoted Sarah.

"We don't know what to pray for – but the Holy Spirit makes intercession (prays for us) according to the will of God (gives direction in the will or to the will of God)," explains Grandpa(+). He continues by saying, "With groanings which cannot be uttered "means the

Holy Spirit takes our inner hurts, tears and problems as if they were really his – and presents them to our Father.

WE OBTAIN HELP IN TIME OF NEED.

"Grandpa, what a lesson! God wants us to approach him by calling him Father - -."

"Daddy," injected Sarah, "and then when we really need help, He sends the Holy Spirit to help us."

"Especially in our prayers," added Sarah.

"Especially in our prayers!" explained Grandpa.

"I'm going to memorize these two verses," stated Tim.

"Me too," echoed Sarah.

"That brings us to what our lesson is about today. It concerns our attitude when we approach God in prayer." (+)

> **With groanings which cannot be uttered means the Holy Spirit takes our inner hurts, tears and problems as if they were really his – and presents them to our Father**

What should be one's attitude in coming before God at the throne of grace in prayer?" inquired Sarah.

THE PROPER ATTITUDE
"Kids notice the statement, **'Our Father which art in heaven**.' What is the next statement?"

Both Sarah and Tim answered in unison, **"HALLOWED BE THY NAME."**

"What do you think that means, **'Hallowed be thy name?'**" Grandpa pauses, and allows his question to sink in.

In a split second both of the young people's hands shot up.

"Does that mean the attitude that one should have when they approach God in prayer?" inquired Sarah. (+)

"Earlier in the chapter Jesus told his disciples that when they prayed that they should enter into a private place and shut the door. Isn't that a commandment to make prayer special by getting alone with God and showing reverence to Him?" asked Tim. (+)

"Grandpa, isn't that kind of like Moses when he met God at the burning bush, and God told him to take his shoes off because he was on holy ground?" offered Sarah.

Grandpa answered, "Who is the teacher in this class? Both of your questions are very good. **Hallowed be thy name is** dealing with the attitude that a person should have when he approaches God in prayer. Hallowed be Thy name, or **may your name be revered, or may your name be held holy, or honored.**" (+)

IT SHOWS HONOR TO GOD

Hallowed be thy name shows honor to the superhuman ruler of the universe. (+) It is more than a subject of a kingdom coming in to the throne room of his human king. **Hallowed be thy name is acknowledging the absolute supremacy of God, who is holy and over all. (+)**

IT ACKNOWLEDGES THE GREATNESS OF GOD

"When Jesus tells us to address the supreme **God of heaven as our 'father' or 'daddy'** and then comments, Hallowed be thy name, that is and expression of love, praise and submission."

THY NAME

"Kids, let's stress, 'Thy Name' from a different view point. We found that John stressed **Father** a total of how many times in the Gospel of John?"

Both young people spoke enthusiastically at about the same time, "146 times."

"Now, lets give a few names, or titles of Jesus, which are found in the Bible. (+) I will illustrate by giving the first."

"Jesus is called, 'The Word'."

Quickly Tim stated, "He is 'Saviour'."

"Good," complimented Grandpa.

"The Rose of Sharon?" Sarah ventured.
"Good," echoed Grandpa.

"He is the Alpha and Omega."

"The Lilly of the Valley."

"The Author and Finisher of our Faith."

"He is the Bright and Morning Star," stated Sarah.

"The Chief Shepherd," was Tim's next title

"The Bridegroom," said Sarah.

"OK kids, you get the point. There are countless titles, or names for Jesus."

"But Grandpa, we just got started," Sarah protested. "**He is the Friend of Sinners,**" she concluded.

"You're absolutely right. There are many, many different titles, or names to describe Jesus. But how many names in the New Testament are there for God?"

> **Hollowed be thy name is** dealing with the attitude that a person should have when he approaches God in prayer. Hallowed be Thy name, or **may your name be revered, or may your name be held holy or honored**

(+) Grandpa just sat there while the children thought.

"He is called Jehovah," said Sarah.

"But that is in the Old Testament," added Tim.

"Hallowed be THY Name," quoted Grandpa. "Kids, it seems to me that God is striving to get his children to center in on one name. 'Father'." (+)

"He is trying to help us to believe in God more than just in a theological sense. He is attempting, by the absence of other titles, to get His children to focus on **the fact that He is our Father**."

"Grandpa, do you mean that now we believe in God, the Father - as the title instead of a person?" inquired Sarah.

"Yes, Sarah, that is exactly what I believe God is trying to emphasize, and get into His children's hearts – 'I am not just a Title – **I am your Heavenly Father'**." (+)

IT SHOWS HUMILITY

"To me, the expression, 'Hallowed be thy name,' shows the attitude one should manifest as he comes to his father in prayer, he should come humbly," instructed Grandpa.

Tim added, "Grandpa that is what the pastor preached on last Sunday. He said, 'God gives grace to the humble'." (I Peter 5:5-6)

"But he resisteth the Proud," added Sarah.

> He is trying to help us to believe in God more than just in a Theological sense. He is attempting, by the absence of other titles, to get His children to focus on **the fact that He is our Father**

Grandpa began to close the lesson by saying, "we have dealt with some very important principles concerning the Model Prayer, which God gave to his disciples to follow..."

"They were given to us to follow also, weren't they, Grandpa?" interrupted Tim.

"They sure were," responded Grandpa.

"But in our next lesson we will come to the heart of the Model Prayer."

"Is that, '**Thy kingdom come**'?" asked Sarah.

"That is your homework assignment in preparation for our next lesson, but let me close this lesson by saying you will never get your prayers answered unless you learn to come in a humble way into the presence of your Heavenly Father. (+) But there is nothing that reveals the praise, reverence and love as the simple approach Jesus gave...." Our Father which are in Heaven... "HALLOWED BE THY NAME."

POINTS TO PONDER

❖ **Almighty God is my Heavenly FATHER.**

❖ **Abba, Daddy, is the dearest term for FATHER.**

❖ **Jesus called God "FATHER" over and over again. (146 times in the Gospel of John alone)**

❖ **Your FATHER gives you the Holy Spirit to help you in time of need.**

❖ **Our FATHER gives grace to the Humble.**

❖ **Our FATHER is more than a Title, He is our FATHER.**

Lesson Four

And it came to pass, that, as he was praying in a certain place, when he ceased, one of his disciples said unto him, LORD, TEACH US TO PRAY, as John also taught his disciples. And he said unto them, WHEN YE PRAY, SAY, Our Father which art in heaven, Hallowed be thy name. THY KINGDOM COME. Thy will be done, as in heaven, so in earth Give us day by day our daily bread. And forgive us our sins; for we also forgive every one that is indebted to us. And lead us not into temptation; but deliver us from evil. Luke 11:1-4

ADDITIONAL SCRIPTURE REFERENCE:
Matthew 6:6-15
Luke 5:5-13

LESSON FOUR

THY KINGDOM COME

"Well, Hello kids," commented Grandpa. "You are a little early aren't you?"

"Grandpa, we weren't able to find anything about **'Thy kingdom come'** so we knew you could help us," was their reply.

"Come on in," smiled grandpa, "I was just joking with you. Now where is that subject found in the Bible?"

"Grandpa, you know. But the first reference you gave me was Luke 11:2, where the apostles ask Jesus to teach them to pray. It is in that verse Jesus said, 'when ye pray SAY'"? replied Tim.(+)

"But we have studied Matthew 6:9 the most, that is where he commanded the apostles, **'after this manner**, pray ye'," said Sarah.

"Kids, I am so glad that you are learning those scriptures so well. It is pretty plain Jesus gave his disciples a model in prayer that He intended them to follow, isn't it?"

THE FIRST THING ON THE PRAYER LIST

"The first request which Jesus gave to the apostles after he had told them how to address their heavenly Father, and in what Spirit to come into his presence, was THY KINGDOM COME. Sarah, remember when you were younger and I would help you write a letter to Santa Clause?" asked Grandpa.

"I remember, but that was when I was little and still believed in Santa Clause." "Yes, I know. But I have a reason for reminding you of those days. What was always the first thing on your list?"

"Why, the most important item, of course. The thing I really, really wanted for Christmas."

THE FIRST THING ON JESUS' LIST

"Sarah, I believe that is the reason that Jesus placed "Thy Kingdom Come" **first on his children's Prayer list."** (+)

"It was the best gift on God's prayer list which would bring all the other blessings."

"In fact, if they didn't understand and pray for the kingdom to come, then they would fail in many of their other prayers also." (+)

"But, Grandpa, I don't ever remember hearing anyone pray for **'Thy Kingdom Come'**," commented Tim.(+)

"What does it mean, Grandpa, **'Thy Kingdom Come'**?" asked Sarah. "What are they praying about?"

"They are praying for the King to come back and begin his millennial reign on this earth," answered Grandpa. (+)

"Jesus is the king! Now, I have heard some people pray about the second coming of Jesus, but I haven't heard anything about a kingdom," commented Tim.

"I have," said Sarah. "Remember the study about the cults we had last summer?"

"Yeah, but the people thought that they would populate their kingdom by having a lot of wives and children. Weren't there two groups that we studied about who didn't believe in hell?" asked Tim.

"Yes," replied Sarah, "but the worst thing about them was, **they did not believe that Jesus was the eternal Son of God,** and the only Savior."

ILLUSTRATION OF A PROBLEM

"Kids, what you said about the cults and their false teaching about the kingdom, reveals the strategy of the devil."

"Really, Grandpa," came the startled reply from the children. "How?"

"The devil has "his" churches teach a lot of false information on the kingdom, so the true preachers will have to focus on the false information in order to refute it to their members. In doing so they focus on the negative, false information, which **helps to blind their minds to the truth of the Bible." (+)**

"The devil has really worked on the minds of people concerning the future millennial kingdom, in order to keep them from seeing **this great motivational truth**."

Sarah asked, "What motivational truth? Grandpa, I really want to understand what Jesus meant when he said, 'Thy Kingdom Come'."

A LITTLE HISTORY LESSON

"Sarah, in order for you to comprehend what Jesus was talking about we must first have a little history lesson."

"Where do we start?" echoed the children.

"We start in the book of Genesis where God states the purpose in man's creation. In Genesis 1:26 the Bible says, 'Let us make man in our image and likeness,' then the verse continues on and gives the purpose for man's creation."

"It reveals that God created Adam and the human race to have **dominion, or rule over the earth**." (+)

When Adam sinned it delayed God's plan, **but it did not change his purpose** of creating man.

In the book of Psalms, King David states that God created man to have dominion over the

---

What do these have in common?

"Seek those things which are above"
"WHEN YE PRAY SAY"
"What I say unto you I say unto all, watch"

They are all commandments of God!

59

work of God's hands. In fact, David said, "Thou hast put all things under his feet." Psalm 8:6

"At Christmas time people often quote Isaiah 9:6, 'For unto us a child is born, unto us a son is given,' and then stop, but the rest of the verse, along with verse seven, tells that Jesus was to be a king and rule the earth. Isaiah 9:6-7 Tim, get your Bible and read those two verses. *'For unto us a child is born, unto us a son is given:* **and the government shall be upon his shoulder:** *and his name shall be called Wonderful Counselor, The Mighty God, The Everlasting Father, The Prince of Peace.* **Of the increase of his government and peace there shall be no end, upon the throne of David, and upon his kingdom,** *to order it, and to establish it with judgment and with justice from henceforth even for ever. The zeal of the Lord of hosts will perform this."* (+) In Revelation 2:26-27, Jesus promises the saints who overcome, that they will have power (authority) over the nations, and will rule them with a rod of iron."

"Does the Bible really say that Grandpa?" Sarah asked.

"Those are the literal words of Jesus," answered Grandpa.

THE SECOND COMING OF CHRIST

"Most Bible believers have heard of the second coming of Christ, but have not connected the second coming with **the beginning of the kingdom**. Jesus announced in Revelation 22:10, 'Behold I come quickly and my reward is with thee, to give every man according as his work shall be'."

Jesus told the apostles to always be watching and ready, because no man knew that exact hour. (+) (Luke 12:40)

The most famous scripture which comforts the hearts of God's people, was given to the apostles on the eve of his crucifixion. He said, "In my father's house are many mansions. I go to prepare a place for you and if I go to prepare a place for you, **I will come again** and receive you unto myself; that where I am, there may you be also.

This caused the early disciples to expect Jesus to come back at any time, which meant they were expecting him come back in their lifetime.

THE SECOND COMING HAS A PURIFYING EFFECT

If a person had a job to finish before the boss came back, and if he didn't know exactly when the boss would return, and if that workman would be rewarded or punished based on whether or not he had his work done then that would keep the workman busy at his task.

That is exactly how Jesus left his disciples; with work to do, and with the knowledge that Jesus could come back at any time.

In First John 3:2, it states that, "*Now we are the Sons of God.*" Then it adds, "*It doth not appear what we shall be* (what kind of bodies) *but we know that when he shall appear, we shall be like him for we shall see him as he is.*"

Now, notice the purifying effect of looking for and expecting Jesus to come back at any time, has on the believer.

In verse three it says, "Every man that hath this hope (expectancy) in him **purifieth himself even as he (Jesus) is pure." (+)**

Sarah's hand shot up.

"Yes?" acknowledged Grandpa.

"What does *purifieth himself* mean?"

"The Bible commands the Christian to 'tithe'. If a child of God expected Jesus to come back, then that Christian wouldn't want Jesus to catch him with the Lord's tithe in his pocket. He would purify himself by giving the Lord's money into the offering. If another Christian had a lost family member, and really expected Jesus to come at any moment, then he would not be passive to that lost family member by living a careless Christian life. He would purify himself by living a dedicated life to the Lord. (+) He would witness to his loved ones.

"Oh, I see," said Sarah.

"That is powerful," commented Tim.

THY KINGDOM COME ADDS POWER

As powerful as living with the imminent coming of Christ in ones mind is; it is not as powerful as living with the coming kingdom in mind.(+)

"I thought you said that looking for his second coming and looking for the coming kingdom were the same," stated Tim.

"No, Tim, they are not the same," corrected Grandpa.

"How are they different," inquired Sarah.

"Looking for the second coming, and to ones reward for faithful service, places the promise of reward in the abstract. Looking for the coming **kingdom**, and the promise of reward, makes the promise of God for faithful service, concrete or absolute. (+)

"Abstract or concrete, Grandpa? That is confusing me. What do you mean?" asked Sarah.

"Sarah, when I say that the promise for faithful service at his second coming is in the abstract, I mean the promise is vague. Like. I will bless you, but the blessing is not spelled out. Some preachers preach, He will reward you for faithful service, but that is in the abstract. It does not reveal what the reward will be."

"But when Jesus talks about the kingdom, he always makes the promise concrete. He reveals exactly what the reward will be."

"Let me illustrate the difference between the abstract promise that some make, and the absolute, or concrete promise, that Jesus makes in the kingdom promises."

Abstract promise—He will bless you.

Concrete promise—I will make you ruler over five cities.

Abstract promise—You will get a reward.

Concrete kingdom promise—I will make you ruler over ten cities.(+)

JUMP AHEAD IN THE MODEL PRAYER

"Now, in order to make this motivating principle even more forceful, we need to read the model prayer.

Sarah, get your Bible and read the model prayer in Matthew 6:10, and stop when I tell you to."

"Thy kingdom come, Thy will be done in earth, as it is in heaven. **Give us this day our daily bread. . . .**" "Stop! Give us what?" asked Grandpa.

"**Our daily bread**," answered Sarah.

"How often are you to pray, if you ask your heavenly father for daily bread?" asked Grandpa.

"**Daily**," repeated both of the children.

> **Abstract promise: He will bless you.**
>
> **Concrete promise: I will make you ruler over five cities.**

There was a pause as Grandpa waited before asking, "If you are to ask God for **DAILY BREAD,** then how often will you have to pray?"

Again both of the young people said, "**Daily**."

"If you pray for daily bread every day, then you would pray, '**Thy kingdom come**,' every day also. That prayer would be **thy kingdom come,** or millennial reign to begin, or the second coming of Jesus to **take place today**. They were to pray for his coming every day." (+)

THE KINGDOM PROMISES TO THE APOSTLES

"Kids, I will reinforce the motivational force of the concrete promise of Jesus concerning the coming kingdom, by giving you a short Bible lesson."

"Good, we are all ears," commented Tim.

"The week before the crucifixion of Jesus, the whole population was talking about the plans of the religious leaders."

"The rulers were seeking someone to deliver Jesus into their hands, so they could kill him. Fear and uncertainty griped most of the population. This caused the large crowds that were in the service of Jesus, to dwindle to just a few people."

"The apostles were concerned about their future, and were discussing what would happen to them if the Jews kill Jesus."

"Jesus knew what the apostles were discussing, so he provoked them to come right out and ask him the question which was on their minds."

In Matthew 19:27 Peter stated, "Behold, we have forsaken all, and followed Thee, **what shall we have therefore (because of this)?**"

Jesus calmly answered Peter by saying, for giving your lives away in order to get people saved in this phase of your life on earth, I will honor you at the Judgment Seat by making you a king over one of the twelve tribes of Israel for 1,000 years.

Read Jesus literal answer in verse 28, where he said, "When the Son of man shall sit on the throne of his glory, ye (the 12 apostles) also shall sit upon twelve thrones, judging the twelve tribes of Israel."

Please note that Peter's question was about a "paycheck", or what they would receive for their dedicated service.(+)

Jesus' answer projected the apostles' minds forward, to the millennial kingdom, where Jesus would sit on King David's throne, and rule over the earth for a thousand years.

He said, when my Kingdom is established, you twelve will be promoted from apostles to kings with each apostle, being king over one of the twelve tribes of Israel.(+)

"Wow, what a paycheck!" exclaimed Tim. "A king for a thousand years."

"But Grandpa, I have a problem. I thought a Christian was to serve the Lord because he loved Jesus, not to get a paycheck or

> Jesus said, when I get my kingdom you twelve will be promoted from apostles to kings with each, king over one of the twelve tribes of Israel.

reward," questioned Sarah.

"That is right Sarah," replied Grandpa. "But how does a Christian prove to Jesus that he really loves him?" questioned Grandpa.

Both of the kids were silent.

In I John 5:3 the Bible declares, "For this is the love of God."

"What is the love of God, John? Is it voicing with one's mouth that you love God? Is it an emotional feeling which causes someone to declare, I love you, God?"

"Whereas both of those could be a way of loving the Lord, but the Bible declares, THIS IS THE LOVE OF GOD THAT WE KEEP HIS COMMANDMENTS."(+)

"Kids, does it cause you to be homesick to see the postman who delivers your mail, when you are on vacation?"

"What?" asked Sarah. "I don't even know my mail carrier, much less miss him when I am on vacation."

"Who do you miss, Sarah?" inquired Grandpa.

"Well, when I was at youth camp last year, Grandpa, and you were sick, I really missed you," answered Sarah.

"You miss the ones like your family. People you really love," replied Tim.

"Exactly," said Grandpa. "Now turn to Luke's gospel and read Luke 22:29-30. Please note what Jesus promises the apostles."

"And I appoint unto you a kingdom, as my Father hath appointed unto me." Now, please note the next few words which Jesus promises the apostles. THAT YE MAY EAT AND DRINK AT MY TABLE. Notice the closeness that the apostles would enjoy with the Savior they loved so dearly." (+)

> Jesus calmly answered Peter's by saying, for giving your lives away in order to get people saved in this phase of your life on earth, I will honor you at the Judgment Seat by making you a king over one of the twelve tribes of Israel for 1,000 years.

The apostles worked hard, and even gave their lives (all except John) as they proved their love to him, by taking the gospel to a lost and dying world. All because they loved him, and wanted to have the close, loving relationship with him for the full thousand years in the millennial kingdom.

"You convince me, Grandpa," commented Tim.

"Wait a minute there young man. I am not through yet," replied Grandpa.

THE APOSTLES WERE NOT CONVERTED YET

"Although Jesus promised those lofty position to the apostles for a full 1,000 years, the apostles were not converted yet!"

"Not converted yet?" came two echoes.

"I'm not talking about becoming a Christian. Sure, all these men were saved. They even rejoiced over his great promise of future reward, but they were not converted to that teaching yet." (+)

"Sarah, quote Psalm 1:2," commanded Grandpa.

He could almost see her mind as it reviewed Psalm 1:1 and then she began to quote verse two.

"But his delight is in the law of the Lord, and in his law **doth he meditate day and night**."

"Well done, Sarah. Thank you," complimented Grandpa.

"I could have done that," offered Tim.

"Sure you could, but I heard Sarah quote Psalm One the other day. Notice the expression; **in his law doth he meditate day and night.**

"What does that mean, Tim?" asked Grandpa.

"Well, when a person meditates on something day and night he thinks about it continually," replied Tim.(+)

Good job. Meditating on a principle, or something in the law of the Lord (Bible), is how the human brain digests something which he heard. Then he continues to think about it over a period of time until **it passes the stage of becoming a conviction**. IT BECOMES PART OF HIM. **He is converted to that principle, which now subsequently directs his life**.

"Do you understand that Sarah?" asked Tim.

"I think so," replied Sarah.

"One becomes converted to a principle through meditation or thinking about it over a period of time." (+)

"Good," responded Grandpa. "We will talk about the specific work that Jesus gave them to do in our next lesson."

"How do you express your love to Jesus, Sarah?" asked Grandpa.

"By keeping his commandments," was her answer.

"What was the great reward that Jesus promised the apostles, Tim?"

"That they would be near him for the full 1,000 years," replied Tim.

"Eat and drink and spend time in his house denoted close fellowship

"How do you express your love to Jesus, Sarah?" asked Grandpa. "By keeping his commandments," was her answer

confirmed Grandpa. (+) No wonder Jesus wanted the apostles to get this beautiful promise in their minds every day by praying, **"Thy-kingdom come"**. IT WAS HIS WAY OF CONVERTING THEM to have a single mind of getting the Gospel to every person on earth and being in a close loving fellowship as they rule and reign over this earth for a 1,000 years. (+)

POINTS TO PONDER

❖ The first thing God wants on His children's prayer list, is "THY KINGDOM COME."

❖ The child of God is to pray, "THY KINGDOM COME" every Day!

❖ "Thy kingdom come" is a Prayer for THE COMING MILLENNIUM.

❖ Praying "Thy kingdom come," lifts the mind off problems of the earth.

❖ Praying "Thy Kingdom come" helps one to live a HOLY LIFE.

❖ "Thy Kingdom come" keeps one LOOKING for the return of Jesus.

Lesson Five

And it came to pass, that, as he was praying in a certain place, when he ceased, one of his disciples said unto him, LORD, TEACH US TO PRAY, as John also taught his disciples. And he said unto them, WHEN YE PRAY, SAY, Our Father which art in heaven, Hallowed be thy name. Thy kingdom come. THY WILL BE DONE, AS IN HEAVEN, so in earth Give us day by day our daily bread. And forgive us our sins; for we also forgive every one that is indebted to us. And lead us not into temptation; but deliver us from evil. Luke 11:1-4

Additional scripture Reference:
Matthew 6:6-15
Luke 5:5-13

LESSON FIVE

THY WILL DONE IN EARTH AS IT IS IN HEAVEN

"It is so good to see you two again. Are you ready for today's lesson?" inquired Grandpa.

"We can hardly wait, Grandpa," came their answer.

"Since I did not give you a homework assignment last time, let me act like a preacher and give you the outline for our study today."

Both of the children nodded their approval and leaned forward with sincere anticipation.

The Second principle in the model prayer is **"Thy (God's) will be done in earth as it is in heaven."**

When one studies this admonition from Jesus, there are four distinct parts of his command.

First, what is the will of God in heaven?

Second, the projected will of God in the earth for the future.

Third, the pronounced will of God in the earth for the present.

Fourth, the personal will of God for each believer's life.

FIRST, WHAT IS THE WILL OF GOD IN HEAVEN?

Thy will be done in earth as it is in heaven. In order to determine what God's will is for the earth, we must first find out **what God's greatest concern and will is in heaven.** (+)

"How can a person ever hope to find that OUT, Grandpa," ask Tim.

Yeah," Sarah said. "That sounds like a pretty difficult, or hopeless task."

"Maybe not, kids," answered Grandpa.

"Grandpa," Tim stated, "Since that is the first point in your outline, please explain how you know what God's Will is in heaven."

OUR CHRISTIAN RESPONSIBILITY
We are found, to find another. We are told, to tell another. We are won, to win another. We are saved, To save another.

"Tim, remember our lesson about God as your heavenly Father?"

"Yes," came Tim's answer.

"Remember how powerful we found Him to be in creating this vast Universe?" (+)

"I'll never forget about Aturas and Hercules and the vast galaxies," answered Sarah.

"And the earth moving in three directions at the same time," added Tim.

"Not only is our Heavenly Father All-powerful but **He is also All-knowing**."

"All-knowing," echoed the children.

"Yes, all-knowing," answered Grandpa.

HEAVEN HAD THE PLAN OF REDEMPTION IN PLACE.

Before Adam's sin and rebellion there was already a plan in place to redeem him. (+)

By God's foreknowledge, He knew that Adam would be tempted by the devil, and would sin. God did not want Adam to sin. He warned him of the awful consequences of sin, but he knew that Adam would sin.

We know what the primary will of heaven is by the actions that had already been taken before Adam's rebellion.

"What action was that, Grandpa?" inquired Tim.

"God had already taken action to redeem sinners from hell, **by placing a perfect plan of salvation in place**."

"Where in the Bible does it say that, Grandpa?" came Sarah's question.

"Sarah, it is the verse following two of your favorite verses in the Bible," answered Grandpa, "quote I Peter 1:18-19."

Sarah complied, "Forasmuch as ye know that ye were not redeemed with corruptible things, as silver and gold, from your vain conversation received by tradition from your fathers; But with the precious blood of Christ, as of a lamb without blemish and without spot:"

The next verse continues, "who (referring to Jesus) was ordained before the foundation of the world, but was manifested in these last times for you."

"Grandpa, those verses say that God knew Adam would sin before He created this world, and had already determined a perfect plan of redemption." marveled Tim.

"Yes, the plan in heaven was that Jesus would leave heaven, and become a man so He could die and pay for man's sin."

"The Lamb denotes Jesus as a perfect, sinless substitute who died to satisfy the broken law that demanded payment," exclaimed grandpa.

"The wages of sin is death," Sarah stated as she understood her grandpa's instruction. "And Jesus died to pay for the sinner's sin in order for God to forgive us." she continued.

"Yes," confirmed Grandpa.   In doing so it revealed **the will of heaven which is to SAVE SINNERS."** (+)

"What a magnificent God we have," exclaimed Tim.

"Yes," agreed Grandpa, "but remember the purpose of this point," he stated. He continued his instruction by repeating, **"Thy will be done IN EARTH as it is in heaven."**

"Then, God's primary will on earth must be to save sinners," agreed the children. (+)

"The primary concern and will of heaven has always been to save sinners," Grandpa stated, "and that is God's greatest concern today. His will for today, on earth as well as in heaven, is to save sinners. That brings us to our second point."

THE PROJECTED WILL OF GOD IN THE EARTH FOR THE FUTURE

Thy will be done on earth as it is in heaven is a prayer for God's future will to be done in the earth. In order to understand what God's will is for the future, one must examine a brief view of God's will as we understand it in heaven.

A PEEK INTO HEAVEN

In heaven God rules as a loving Father. There is no pain, tears, anxiety, sickness, death or sorrow. (+)

One of my favorite hymns describes heaven as a place where **"all is joy and peace and love and the soul of man shall never die."**

God, our loving Father, is the object of praise, worship, and adoration. (+) The fellowship of heaven is not broken by anything, and the joyful anticipation of destroying the devil in hell, and righting all wrongs on earth by the return of King Jesus to the earth ,grows every day.

> Those verses say that God knew Adam would sin before He created this world, and had already determined a perfect plan of redemption

It is a perfect paradise, and the greatest joy of God is to bless and delight his happy family.(+)

With this feeble attempt to peek into, and reveal God's happy home in heaven, we are to pray daily, "Thy will be done **IN EARTH** as it is in heaven."

A PROMISE OF PEACE AND GOD'S WILL

The prophet Isaiah foresaw the birth of a child who is the prince of peace, and who would establish a kingdom on this earth in which there would be no end. Isaiah 9:6-7

> **What do these have in common?**
>
> "Look unto me and be ye saved"
> "WHEN YE PRAY SAY"
> "Go, ye into all the world and preach"
>
> **They are all commandments of God!**

Daniel revealed the history of all major ruling kingdoms on this earth, with the promise that when Jesus comes back to the earth he will establish a kingdom which shall stand forever. (Daniel 2:44) The vivid language of Daniel reveals that God will right all wrongs, and **personally implement his reign on earth as it is in heaven. (+)**

One of his first acts will be to chain the devil and put him into hell. Revelation 20:1-2 states, "The Devil and Satan, and bound him a thousand years and cast him into the bottomless pit and shut him up."

He will judge all nations, and the promise of the angels at his birth will finally become a reality.

They sang, "Glory to God in the highest, and on earth, peace and good will toward men." Luke 2:14.

A PRAYER ANSWERED

In Isaiah chapter eleven, we have many of the conditions which will prevail on this earth when King Jesus comes back.

The curse is taken from the earth and animal kingdom. Verse 6-7. Isaiah 62:25

There will be no death – Isaiah 65:20, no wars – Isaiah 2:4, and no tears – Isaiah 65:19.

They shall not hurt or destroy in all my holy mountain, for the earth shall be **full of the knowledge of the Lord** as the waters cover the seas. Isaiah 11:9.(+)

The prayer of "**thy will be done in earth as it is in heaven**" will finally be answered, and the eternal purpose of God for man to have dominion over the earth, will finally become a reality.

"Whew, Grandpa, you really got to preaching there," reported Sarah.

"Amen to that," stated Tim. "What a mighty God we serve."

THIRD, THE PRONOUNCED WILL OF GOD FOR THE PRESENT

God is more concerned about the present than he is about the future. (+) "What is the will of God **on this earth today?"**

"Sarah, why did Jesus come to the earth?"

"To die," she answered.

"For whom?" Grandpa continued.

"For sinners," Tim answered.

"Why did he die for sinners?" continued Grandpa.

"To save them, us, from hell," replied the children.

In fact, we don't have to guess or wonder why Jesus came to the earth. Listen to the very words of Jesus from his own lips, as to why he came to this earth," **For the Son of man (Jesus) is come to seek and to save that which is lost." Luke 19:10. (+)**

We do not have to wonder what heaven's will is concerning the salvation of the lost.

God stated that he was not willing that any should perish, and then proved his great love by sending his Son into the world to die on the cross.

John 3:16, the golden verse of the Bible, declares God's great love and provision for sinners.(+)

The commission of Jesus to his church is to go to every creature, in every nation beginning at Jerusalem, and preach the gospel (God's good news). That God's will is "whosoever that will call upon the name of the Lord shall be saved." (+)

Follow the personal ministry of Jesus on the earth as he wins souls in his daily life. Note some of the people and the places where Jesus won souls in his daily life:

- ❖ He won Nicodemus, a ruler of the Jews at night in Jerusalem; John 5
- ❖ He won a fallen women at Jacob's well at noon; John 4
- ❖ He won a hopeless sinner in the graveyard; Mark 5
- ❖ He won the blind man on the Sabbath day; John 9
- ❖ He won the woman taken in adultery; John 8
- ❖ He won a little crook, Zaccheus, up a tree
- ❖ He took time in his suffering on the cross to save the thief.

Jesus went everywhere, and wherever he went he won souls," commented Tim.

"Aren't the people you named the better known cases of soul-winning, Grandpa," said Sarah.

> **For the Son of man (Jesus) is come to seek and to save that which is lost." Luke 19:10**

"Yes, Sarah what Tim said is so true, and a vivid description of the Daily Life of Jesus. Jesus went everywhere, and wherever he went he won sinners," summarized Grandpa. (+) One can see the will of God on this earth by focusing on what Emmanuel (God in the flesh) did while he was on the earth. His eternal passion is to save sinners from eternal ruin and destruction in hell (+)

Paul understood what the model prayer meant when it said, 'Thy will be done in earth as it is in heaven'. He said that he became "all things to all men, that I might by all means save some (from Hell)." I Corinthians 9:22.

God's primary will on earth in our present day is to save sinners.

FOURTH, THE PERSONAL WILL OF GOD FOR EACH BELIEVER'S LIFE

This is the very thing that every person is wondering about — "What is God's will for my life?"(+)

"Grandpa, that is one of my great concerns," confessed Tim.

"Me too," agreed Sarah.

"They even give aptitude tests in high school to help kids find out what vocation they are best fitted for," said Tim.(+)

"God placed a book in the Bible that answers that question," informed Grandpa.

"Really!" exclaimed Tim.

"Which one?" asked Sarah.

"It is the book of Ecclesiastes. God inspired Solomon, the richest and wisest man of his day to conduct an experiment to find out why God placed men on the earth." Note Solomon's words; he was to, "see what was that good for the sons of men, which **they should do under the heaven all the days of their lives.**"(Ecclesiastes 2:13)

> Paul understood what the model prayer meant when it said, 'Thy will be done in earth as it is in heaven'. He said that he became "all things to all men, that I might by all means save some (from Hell)."

Solomon tried experiment after experiment until he experimented with every facet of life. (+) **He tried labor – he tried laughter. He tried luxury. He tried lust**. After each experiment he would give the summary of his finding. He reported that all those things didn't satisfy the human heart. Finally in the last two verses of the book of Ecclesiastes, he gave the purpose of man on this earth - "Let us hear the conclusion of the whole matter; Fear God, and keep his commandments: for this is the whole duty of man. For God shall bring every work into judgment, with every secret thing, whether it be good, or, whether it be evil." Ecclesiastes 12:13 - 14

From his experiment He gave the primary purpose for each Christian on the earth. His finding and wise council to God's purpose and will is summed up in Proverbs 11:30, "The fruit of the righteous is a tree of life; and he that winneth souls is wise." (+)

SOLOMON GAVE THE PRIORITIES OF LIFE

It is obvious that Solomon understood the priorities of God for his life.

It was first a preacher or a soul-winner.

It was second, the son of King David.

The final vocation was king in Jerusalem, one can read Solomon's declaration of priorities in Ecclesiastes 1:1

"The words of the preacher (Solomon) the Son of David, king in Jerusalem,"

First, preacher or soul-winner.

Second, son of one of God's greatest servants.

Third, king in Jerusalem.

His spiritual obligation to God first, his family second, and his job third. (+)

> *"Let us hear the conclusion of the whole matter; Fear God, and keep his commandments: for this is the whole duty of man. For God shall bring every work into judgment, with every secret thing, whether it be good, or, whether it be evil." Ecclesiastes. 12:13 - 14*

A REMINDER, EVERY DAY

The apostles had a reminder every day of what God's will for their lives was. The model prayer which they were commanded to pray everyday - "**Thy will be done in earth as it is in heaven**" was their daily reminder. (+)

"Grandpa, I have a question," asked Sarah.

"What is that, Sarah?" answered Grandpa.

"Do you think that the average member in our church thinks about winning souls?" (+)

"I know that until our Bible studies, I never thought it was God's will for my life to win souls," stated Tim.

Grandpa paused as he looked at the children. The seriousness in their faces touched his heart as he cleared his thoughts and simply stated, "You can see now why we must follow Jesus' model in learning to pray." (+)

JESUS DECLARES MAN'S PRIMARY PURPOSE

In concluding our lesson on "**Thy will be done in earth as it is in heaven**," let's let Jesus have the final word.

"As my Father hath sent me into the world, even so send I you." John 20:21 (+)

Again, why did Jesus come into the world?

"To seek and to save sinners," Grandpa confirmed. "Let us use the wisdom of Solomon to establish our life's priorities."

It is God's business first, soul-winning.

It is our family second.

And it is our vocation third.

The clear teaching of God's will for the believer's life is to win people from hell.

> **Night Watch**
> **By Dorothy M Struthers**
>
> Lord, I am tired!
> The day's been hard;
> The foe provoked me long.
> I used Thy Sword
> I walked by faith
> To battle deadly wrong.
>
> Now I am weak,
> By sleep o'ercome.
> I wait with failing sight.
> But I'll not fear
> For this I know-
> Lord, you'll watch through the night!

"Kids join me as we pray, Oh God, may thy will be done in out lives in earth as thy will is done in heaven."

REWARDING SERVICE

Once when William E. Gladstone was facing one of the great crises of his political life, he sat writing one morning at two o'clock the speech with which he hoped to win a great political victory In the House of Commons the next day. At that hour there came to his door the mother of a poor, friendless, dying cripple, and besought him to come and bring some message of hope and cheer to the hopeless boy.

And without hesitation the great commoner left the preparation of his speech, spent the night leading the child to Christ. He then went back to his home, and faced his day with a smile of confidence and peace and power. In that hour he said to a friend, "I am the happiest man in the world today." He had been able to serve a little child in a tenement house in the name of the Master.
-From Men and the Kingdom.

POINTS TO PONDER

❖ God's will on this earth was determined before Adam sinned.

❖ The proper priority in a Christian's life should be:
    o   God's Work First.
    o   Family Second
    o   Job Third

❖ God wants to save sinners so much that He gave His Son on the cross.

❖ Jesus came to seek and to save sinners.

❖ As my Father sent me into the world even so send I you.

❖ My purpose and God's will on this earth is to save sinners.

Lesson Six

After this manner therefore pray ye: Our Father which art in heaven, Hallowed be thy name. Thy kingdom come. Thy will be done in earth, as[it is in heaven. GIVE US THIS DAY OUR DAILY BREAD. And forgive us our debts, as we forgive our debtors. And lead us not into temptation, but deliver us from evil: For thine is the kingdom, and the power, and the glory, forever.
AMEN.
Matthew 6:9-13

Additional scripture Reference:
Matthew 6:6-15
Luke 5:5-13

LESSON SIX

GIVE US THIS DAY OUR DAILY BREAD

"Hello, there.   How are two of my favorite people today?" welcomed Grandpa as the children seated themselves around his desk in the study.

"We are great," answered Tim.

"We are with our favorite Grandpa and teacher," responded Sarah.

"Good!   Today's lesson is a lesson that is directed toward the three of us in our daily lives."

"Give us this day our daily bread" or as Dr. Luke recorded it **"Give us day by day our daily bread."** (+)

DOES ANYONE PRAY THAT WAY

"Grandpa, as Sarah and I were walking over here we were discussing our lesson today."

"Good," exclaimed Grandpa.

"And we were wondering, does anyone pray that way today?" (+)

"What way?" inquired Grandpa.

"You know," replied Sarah, "Give us day by day our daily bread."

"We don't know anyone who prays that way," concluded Tim.

"Yes Tim, there are many who look to God everyday to supply their Daily needs. One of the most famous people who prayed that way was George Muller.

"I heard of him. Wasn't he a preacher who lived in England, and has a big orphanage?" inquired Sarah. "There is a book about him in the church library."

"Yes, that's the man, and I would encourage anyone to get that book and read it. It will help increase your faith."

"What did he do that was so great, Grandpa?" questioned Tim.

"He built an orphanage in Bristol, England that fed and educated thousands of orphans. When he turned the orphanage over to his staff at the age of 72, they had over 2200 orphans living there. He prayed everyday, and never once ask people for money or food. He did it in obedience to, "give us day by day our daily bread." He started out as a poor obscured preacher with one or two orphans who lived with he and his family, and **through prayer and prayer only**, he built the buildings, paid the staff and fed over 2000 children daily. (+)

"And that was about 200 years ago wasn't it Grandpa?" inquired Sarah.

"Yes it was, and another amazing thing about George Muller, he raised millions of dollars to give to other missionaries while running the orphanage."

"All by prayer?" Tim questioned.

"All by prayer," answered Grandpa, "Tim, there was a young man, a little older than you that dedicated himself to following this model prayer and pray, **'Give us day by day our daily bread'**. Although his parents were quite well to do, he refused to let them help him as he went to college. He often would go almost without food for a period of time, before the old doctor whom he worked for would pay him.

"Why on earth would he do that Grandpa?" inquired Sarah with surprise.

"God had called him to China as a missionary. Young Hudson reasoned, "I had better learn to move God's hand by prayer in friendly England where I can communicate in English, than to wait until I get to China where I know no one, and cannot speak their language," explained Grandpa.

"Was that Hudson Taylor Grandpa? They also have a book about him in the church library." Inquired Sarah.

"Yes Hudson Taylor changed China through practicing, **Give us day by day our daily bread**." (+) He lived in China for seven years before he had his first convert. Through great difficulties, before the end of his life he had translated the Bible into the Chinese language, had thousands saved and through prayer over 1100 missionaries were called, and went to China."

"All through prayer?" questioned the young people.

"All through prayer," answered Grandpa. "**You would be surprised** how many young people put themselves through college by prayer today." (+)

"Thank you, Grandpa. That's helped a lot," announced Sarah.

TEACH US TO WALK BY FAITH

His instruction to us to look to him each day for our daily bread, is God's way of teaching us to **walk by faith.** (+) We have God's vivid example of supplying upward to two million Jews their daily bread (manna) for 40 years, to show his great ability. So taking care of the three of us should not be that difficult.

> There is no time lost in waiting, if you are waiting on the Lord.

"Sarah, turn to Matthew 6:33 and read that verse for us," requested Grandpa. Why don't you let my big brother quote it for you," suggested Sarah.

With that Tim began, "But seek ye first the kingdom of God and his righteousness and all these things shall be added unto you." (+)

"What things is he talking about, Grandpa?" asked Sarah.

"When one reads verses 26 through 32 he finds that Jesus used the birds as examples of creatures which he fed or provided for. These birds did not sow or harvest a crop, but depended totally upon God to take care of them. Then Jesus asked the question, "**Are ye not much better than they**?" (Verse 26)

In the following verses, God declares that he clothed the flowers who did nothing to clothe themselves. Then he commented that the rich king, Solomon, was not clothed as beautifully as the flowers.

"Is, food and clothing the '**all things**' which God promises to those that seek first the kingdom of God and his righteousness?" inquired Tim.

"You got it Tim. That is exactly what God is promising," answered Grandpa.

"What does 'seek first the kingdom of God and his righteousness' mean, Grandpa?" inquired Sarah.

"It means putting God and his will for us on this earth before our own desires and pleasures, doesn't it Grandpa?" Tim answered. (+)

We have God's vivid example of supplying upward to two million Jews their daily bread (manna) for 40 years to show his great ability. So taking care of the three of us should not be that difficult.

"Yes, Tim, God promises that if we will seek God's will and live for him, that He (God) will in turn supply all our needs, which includes food and clothing."

"Otherwise, if one will live by the

94

principles of the Bible and wins souls, then God will take care of all his needs.

Have I got the right understanding of that verse, Grandpa?" inquired Sarah.

"Yes, Sarah, your grandmother and I have found in our life together over the past 40 years, that God will keep his Word. But let me confess, it was not always easy. But God always came through and kept His Word." (+)

"So you enter into a partnership with God by saying, 'God, I am going to put the kingdom of God and your righteousness first, and then expect you to take care of my needs." Is that what God is promising in these verses, Grandpa?" Tim asked in a serious tone.

Yes, Tim, that is what God is promising, and that is what is called **walking by faith. (+)**

TEACH US TO TRUST GOD'S WORD

"Tim, do you know what an immutable promise is?" asked Grandpa.

"No, Grandpa. I've never heard that word before."

"Sarah, how about you."

"How do you spell it?" Sarah asked,

"I-M-M-U-T-A-B-L-E, immutable," answered Grandpa.

"No," replied Sarah.

"How about the word unalterable?"

"Grandpa, just breaking down the word unalterable reveals its meaning. Something which can not be altered."

Grandpa continued his questions, "How about the word unchangeable? That's something which can't be changed," responded Sarah.

"Right," replied Grandpa. "How about the word, irrevocable?" "Something which cannot be revoked or changed?" asked Tim.

"Yes, Tim and these three words are **synonyms for immutable.**"

"Immutable means unchangeable, unalterable or something that cannot be revoked." (+)

TWO IMMUTABLE PRINCIPLES

God wants his children to believe him and trust his promises so he gave not one, **but two immutable principles.**

Number one, the first immutable principle is, **GOD CANNOT LIE! (+)**

The Holy, righteous God of truth cannot lie. IT is against his nature. He is absolutely holy, and cannot lie. Hebrew 6:18 states, "That by two immutable things, in which it was impossible for God to lie....."

And Two, God swore upon his honor that he will not lie. (+)

There are many ways that people tell lies or untruths.

Some people deliberately tell a half-true or out-and-out-lie. Some people have the absolute determination to keep their word and perform their promise, but something happens which causes them to break their word. The car wouldn't start, or someone came by or their promise just slipped their mind. Other times, it was more difficult than they thought it would be, and they did their best but failed because of human weakness. BUT GOD DOES NOT HAVE ANY OF THOSE PROBLEMS. He knows when he states the promise that he can perform and keep his WORD.(+) In order to make people know that he meant the promise, he took an oath on his honor that he would do it.(+)

"Tim, please turn to Hebrews 6:17 for us."

"Wherein God, willing more abundantly to shew unto the heirs of promise the immutability of his counsel, confirmed it by an oath:

"Sarah, remember last week when I promised you that I would pick you up at school at 3:30. **I lied to you.**"

"Oh, Grandpa, you didn't know there would be a bad accident between your house and the school that would make you late," scolded Sarah.

What do these have in common?

"The just shall live by faith"
"WHEN YE PRAY SAY"
"Believe on the Lord Jesus Christ and thou shalt be saved"

They are all commandments of God!

"That's my point, Sarah. **God knows all things**. He can foresee all circumstances and he has unlimited power. When he makes a promise he knows all things, all hindrances, and all elements, and knows that HE HASN'T OVERSTATED WHAT HE COULD AND WOULD DO."

"First, God cannot lie. Second, he took an oath that he is fully aware of all circumstances, and that he would perform his word and keep his promises."

"God promised David, 'My covenant will I not break nor alter the thing that is gone out of my lips.' Psalm 89:34."

"Tim, when you read in the Bible a promise God makes, you can rest assured that God will keep His promise."

ALL THIRTY THOUSAND OF THEM

"All thirty thousand of them," commented Tim

"Of what?" inquired Sarah.

"His promises. That's what I read in a sermon book the other day. The author stated that there was 30,000 promises of God in the Bible. (+)"

"After studying about Antares and Hercules, and the vastness of our Universe, I can believe it," said Sarah.

"I've heard that figure also, Tim. I don't know how anyone could determine how many promises God made in the Bible, but I know one thing. . . ." stated Grandpa.

"What's that, Grandpa?" asked Sarah.

"Every promise he made, he will keep because of these two immutable principles. (+)

"First, because God cannot lie"

"And second, God took an oath upon his own honor that he would not lie or alter his promise."

TEACH US TO HANG ONTO HIS PROMISES

Even though God goes to such great lengths to get us to trust him and walk by faith, at times, it will not be easy.

Peter warned that there were fiery trials in every Christian's life which were designed to test and strengthen his faith. (+)

I Peter 4:12 – 13 says that we are to rejoice if we are reproached by people because we are living for Christ. This is a sure sign that we are pleasing Him and will lead to Spiritual growth and will glorify Christ.

Peter states that we grow in faith by adding to our faith virtue, and to virtue (good Christian habits) knowledge, etc. I Peter 1:4-5. As we add these Christian traits in our life we grow in faith and become more like Jesus.

Paul stated that we are to grow in faith. Then he gives the secret of growing in our ability to trust the promises of God. He said, **"Faith comes by hearing, and hearing by the Word of God."** Romans 10:17. (+)

Both Peter and Paul affirmed that one grows in ability to trust the Lord by hearing the Word of God. As one hears the Word of God He begins to believe it.

Believing the Word of God causes one to act upon it.

Practicing the Word of God and obeying it they learn to walk by faith and please their Heavenly Father. Heb. 11:6. The process of walking by faith was an on going effort in the Life of Abraham, until he became known as the Father of the faithful. (+) He continued to grow in faith through out his life time.

GIVE US SOME SIMPLE STEPS

"Grandpa, I sure have learned a lot from today's lesson, but can you give us some simple steps in growing in faith," Tim inquired.

"Yes, remember, we are just starting out in our walk of faith. What are the first steps, so to speak, in our walk of faith?"

LOOK TO YOUR FATHER AS YOU PRAY THE MODEL PRAYER

The first step in learning to walk by faith is to obey Jesus' command to the apostles. He said, when ye pray, **say**. Follow the model prayer everyday so you learn to live your life in the light of eternity, and the soon coming of Christ.

LOOK TO YOUR FATHER AND
CLAIM HIS COVENANT

The verse you quoted Tim, Matt. 6:33, is God's offered covenant with his children. (+) God has stated that it is his GOOD pleasure to give to his children liberally. (Luke 12:31-32) Meet the conditions of always putting him first and depend upon him to supply your needs.

LOOK TO YOUR FATHER AS YOUR SILENT
PARTNER

God gives us **all**; our strength, our life, our ability to think and reason. Jesus told the apostles very plainly, "Without me, ye can do nothing."

He equips and gives strength to earn income, and his desire is that we do well. He offers to go into business with us as OUR SILENT PARTNER.

The proposal he offers is – I will give you desire, favor and ability to make 100% of your earnings. The deal I make with all of my children is for them to dedicate the first 10% back to me, so I can lay it up in the Bank of Heaven as an eternal investment for them. God tells all of his children, if you will **trust me as your money manager,** I promise to make the rest of the 90% go farther than the 100% would if you had kept it all. (+) This promise is made plain in Malachi 3:10. Bear in mind that "tithe" means 10%. Also note that God challenges his children by saying, **"Prove me now!"** Malachi 3:10 "Kids, one of the first steps in learning to walk by faith is to trust the Lord by following the Bible's plan of giving.

LOOK TO YOUR FATHER TO MAKE
YOU FRUITFUL

Every living thing that God placed on this earth was for the same purpose. It was to bear fruit or be productive. In the book of Genesis He makes it clear that everything is to reproduce **after it's kind**. This principle governs the spiritual realm also. Everyone who receives Christ as his Savior is to be fruitful and reproduce himself by winning souls.

Solomon taught that the fruit of the righteous (saved) is a tree of life producing fruit (to others) and he that winneth souls is wise. Proverbs 11:30

God made a bold statement that anyone can win souls if, **They by faith, follow God's laws of a sure harvest.** This rule of a sure harvest is found in Psalm 126:5-6. Verse five deals with the heart and soul of soul-winning when it states, "They (anyone) that sow (give the word) in tears (burdened heart) will reap (win souls) in Joy." (+)

Then he gives the principles of a sure harvest in verse six. Note, They are:

Going – He that goeth forth
Weeping – with a burdened heart
Sowing – bearing precious seed (message)
Believing – shall doubtless come again
Rejoicing – Rejoicing as he brings his fruit.

If a person goes in faith, looking to his Father, then his Father's promise of making him fruitful will happen. It may not happen the first time he goes, but if he will be faithful in going he will become fruitful. We have God's immutable promise for it.

LOOK TO YOUR FATHER
FOR ABUNDANCE

Your big God or powerful Dad wants his children to excel abundantly. (+) Jesus stated that the reason he came into the world was so people could have life (be saved) and **have life more abundantly**. John 10:10

> God tells all of his children, if you will **trust me as your money manager,** I promise to make the rest of the 90% go farther than the 100% would if you had kept it all.

"Now, Tim, as we close this simple little lesson turn to II Corinthians. 9:6-8 and read it for us," requested Grandpa.

"But this I say, He which soweth sparingly shall reap also sparingly; and he which soweth bountifully shall reap also bountifully. Every man according as he purposeth in his heart, so let him give; not grudgingly, or of necessity: for God loveth a cheerful giver. And **God is able to make all grace abound toward you**; that ye, always having all sufficiency in all things, may abound to every good work:"

"Notice how to have an abundant life:

SOW ABUNDANT SEED IN GIVING AND
SERVING AND ONE WILL HAVE

A great life
A full and joyful life
A rich and rewarding millennium

103

SOW SELF-CENTERED SEEDS FOR SELF GRATIFICATION AND ONE WILL HAVE

A struggling life
A life full of regrets
A tragic millennium

"Kids, whether you live a full, happy life or a poor struggling life will depend on your obeying, **give us this day our daily bread** and live a life of faith."

TEACH US TO OBEY GOD'S WORD

In the model prayer Jesus is saying all of the above when he teaches us to pray…

Dear heavenly Father, or Our dear daddy.

Who enjoys feeding the birds and clothing the beautiful flowers?

Who promises that he who cannot lie and took an oath on his own honor that he would not lie. Our loving Father who promises his children that if we put him and his righteous will first in our lives that **he will feed, clothe, and answer our prayers.**

Oh wonderful, loving Father who controls all the vast universe and knows our every need.

Give this day our daily bread and help us to please you by walking and living, **by faith. (+)**

AMEN

POINTS TO PONDER

❖ Jesus commanded us to pray everyday for our DAILY possessions.

❖ It is our Father's good pleasure to supply our daily needs.

❖ Abraham grew from being a common man to the father of faith.

❖ It is God's way of helping to increase our faith.

Lesson Seven

After this manner THEREFORE PRAY YE: Our Father which art in heaven, Hallowed be thy name. Thy kingdom come. Thy will be done in earth, as it is in heaven. Give us this day our daily bread. And FORGIVE US OUR DEBTS, AS WE FORGIVE OUR DEBTORS. And lead us not into temptation, but deliver us from evil: For thine is the kingdom, and the power, and the glory, forever. Amen. FOR IF YE FORGIVE MEN THEIR TRESPASSES, YOUR HEAVENLY FATHER WILL ALSO FORGIVE YOU: BUT IF YE FORGIVE NOT MEN THEIR TRESPASSES, NEITHER WILL YOUR FATHER FORGIVE YOUR TRESPASSES
-Matthew 6:9-15

LESSON SEVEN

FORGIVE US OUR DEBTS AS WE FORGIVE OUR DEBTORS

"Hello, Tim, Sarah, it is good to see you," called out Grandpa as he saw his two young students come up on the porch.

Each of the two replied, and Grandpa began the lesson by saying, "Today, our lesson is about preventive medicine." (+) This statement brought their startled responses.

"Grandpa, aren't we going to have our lesson on prayer today?" Sarah asked.

"You got another reader's digest joke for us today?" inquired Tim.

"No, I'm not kidding," replied Grandpa. "In fact, I am dead serious. I wouldn't joke about the deadly spiritual cancer that is destroying so many people today. In fact, this is more deadly than cancer, and much more destructive."

"Yes, Sarah, our lesson is on prayer today. Matthew states the part of the model prayer that we find in our lesson by saying, "**Forgive us our debt as we forgive our debtors.** Dr. Luke is more pointed in saying, "Forgive us our sins; for we also forgive every one who is indebted unto us." (+)

THE MODEL PRAYER ORDER OF REQUESTS

Most people in our modern day teach that the first thing one should pray for after addressing God, should be the forgiveness of one's sins. No doubt this is exactly what one should do if they are not totally dedicated to God. But the forgiveness of one's sins is found fourth on God's prayer list in our study.

Remember **lesson one** explains the difference between the model prayer and the Lord's Prayer. (+)

"Yes," injected Tim, "and before the model there is a command from Jesus who commanded, **when ye pray say!**"

"**Lesson two** dealt with the recognition of the all powerful, all knowing, and all present God of heaven as our Father or Daddy," continued Grandpa.

"**Lesson three** gives the attitude of reverence one should have in addressing God in prayer."

"**Lesson four** deals with "thy kingdom come" which was placed in the model prayer to be prayed every day, in order to motivate and purify the Christian to live a holy life."

"**Lesson five** makes God's people see that God's will on earth in our day is for each Christian to win souls."

"**Lesson six** taught that each child of God is to walk by faith, as he depends upon God for his daily bread." (+)

"Tim, if God's people would follow these instructions which are listed in the model prayer, what type of effect would it have upon them?" asked Grandpa.

"That's easy, Grandpa," piped in Sarah. "They would live Holy lives."

"She's right," commented Tim. "If people were thinking of God as their Father, and were humbly coming into his presence on a daily basis, looking for and praying for God's millennial kingdom to begin, they would be trusting the Lord and trying to please him in everything they do." (+)

"They wouldn't have a big sin problem would they kids? Their minds would be consumed on God's will and upon their service for Him. Do you see how learning to pray right would create a right attitude to God, and help them to live, a more spiritual life, and cause people to have less problems with sin?

What do these have in common?
"Thou shalt love the Lord with all thy heart"
"WHEN YE PRAY SAY"
"Seek first the kingdom of God"

They are all commandments of God!

GOD'S ABSOLUTE PROMISE OF FORGIVENESS

"Regardless of where one places the forgiveness of one's sins on the list, God has promised..."

"And his promises are immutable," injected Sarah, showing off her knowledge of a new word.

Grandpa smiled and continued, "If a child of God confesses his sins then God is just and faithful to forgive us our sins and cleanse us from all unrighteousness." I John 1:9. (+)

It is vital that a Christian keeps a clean heart before God in order to get his prayers answered.

The Psalmist reveals that if a believer regards iniquity (sin) in his heart then God will not answer his prayers. (+) Ps. 66:18

LORD, TEACH US TO PRAY

The very request that the disciples made to Jesus, "Lord, teach us to pray," reveals that Jesus not only gave instructions on how to pray, **but why they should pray that way. (+)**

Sarah's hand went up. "Grandpa, I have a question."

"Yes, what is it, Sarah?"

"Jesus gave comments on what he was teaching them about prayer just the way you are teaching us?"

"You have the right idea Sarah, but I am doing a poor job compared to the job Jesus did."

"Now, the reason I am drawing attention to his teaching on the model prayer, is **it must have taken** several sessions for him to explain **the why and how** behind every principle in the model prayer."

"It sure has taken us quite a bit of time and we are not through yet, Grandpa," agreed Tim.

"Most of what he taught was not recorded in the Bible, so when you find comments which he felt were so important that he included them in the Bible, those **comments must be very important.**"

"Turn in your Bible to Matthew 6:14-15, which are the first two verses after the model prayer, and we will study one of those comments on prayer. In verse 14 Jesus warned the disciples that if THEY DID NOT FORGIVE MEN THEIR TRESPASSES THEN GOD WOULD NOT FORGIVE THE APOSTLES THEIR SINS." (+)

"What would happen, Grandpa, if God wouldn't forgive a child of God their sins?" asked Tim.

"The first thing that would happen is the close fellowship with God **would be broken.**"

"They would feel guilty and would not have any joy, would they Grandpa?" offered Sarah.

"Yes, Sarah, they would not break the relationship with God. They would still be his children, but **it would quench their fellowship.**" (+)

THE DESTRUCTION OF BITTERNESS

"It would also cause the one who was offended to develop a wrong attitude toward the offender. (+) If they continued in their unforgiveness to the offender then they would become suspicious of the offender's motive, and soon they would become critical of his actions."(+)

"This would cause God to begin a corrective action designed to lead the person with the unforgiving spirit to repent of their sin of unforgiveness. If he didn't repent, then his heart would soon become hardened toward God." (+)

"Their spiritual life would continue to dry up because their fellowship with God was declining. They would no longer feel his loving presence. Their unforgiving spirit **would soon turn into bitterness**."(+) "Bitterness would cause them to become hardened and cold." (+)

"I see, I see!" cried Sarah.

"You see what?" inquired Tim.

"I see what Grandpa meant when he said that we were going to study preventive medicine."

"I understand it also Grandpa, but why did Jesus teach them to pray that way?"

"What way, Tim?"

"Well," he said, "**Forgive us our debts** or sins and we forgive our debtors? What does he mean *debtors*?"

PEOPLE HAVE CERTAIN RESPONSIBILITIES AND OBLIGATIONS

"God has given people certain duties and responsibilities in life. For instance, fathers are to supply the physical needs of their families. Fathers owe their families that, and **it's a debt they should pay**. Parents are responsible for the training and for the welfare of their children. According to God's Word, parents owe their children training and a sense of well being. Husbands are commanded to love their wives and treat them with love and respect." (+)

"When husbands fail to do that, their wives are hurt or offended. **The debt the husbands owe was not paid.**"

"Parents live selfish or self-centered lives and neglect their children, which causes the children to be lonely or offended at their parents. **Parents did not pay the debt that they owed their children.**"

"People lie or tell half-truths about friends and family members, when, according to the Bible **they owe them the truth.**"

"People embarrass others by things they say or do."

TWO CATEGORIES OF SIN

"There are two categories of sin," Grandpa stated.

"Like good sins and bad sins?" questioned Sarah.

Their spiritual life would continue to dry up because their fellowship with God was declining. They would no longer feel his loving presence. Their unforgiving spirit **would soon turn into bitterness**. Bitterness would cause them to become hardened and cold.

113

"There are no good sins, according to the Bible are there Grandpa?" Tim quickly asked.

"I am not talking in a Theological sense right now kids. I am trying to get you to think."

"Well, you have aroused our curiosity, Grandpa," was their response.

"People think of sin as some action like murder, stealing, or deliberately hurting someone. But there are many sins that are worse that even people who are considered to be good Christians commit."

"The world has a way of classifying sins as to which are bad and which are not so bad," Grandpa continued. (+) "They all make the same deductions, which are wrong."

"Worse?" exclaimed Sarah "Than murder?" continued Tim.

"Yes," replied Grandpa as he sat there to let his answer sink in.

"You are my Grandpa and I believe what you say, but a sin that is worse than murder?" stated Sarah.

"Sarah, I know Grandpa has something up his sleeve. It must have something to do with the two categories of sin."

> People think of sin as some action like murder, stealing, or deliberately hurting someone. But there are many sins that are worse, that even people who are considered to be good Christians commit."

"What are the two categories of sin Grandpa?" asked Sarah.

"Let me ask you another question before answering yours, Sarah. If God commands a person to do something and the person doesn't do it, is that sin?"

"Yes," was her answer.

"Sarah, we would call that 'SIN OF OMISSION.'"

"Omission and the sin of Commission," injected Tim. "The two classes of sin are the ones people commit, and the commands they omit or fail to do." **"The sin of Omission and the sin of Commission,"** offered Sarah. "Is that right, Grandpa?"

"You are right Sarah. Now, let me ask you another question. Which is the worst sin? The sin of omission or the sin of commission?" Asked Grandpa. (+)

"The sin of commission, naturally," came Sarah's answer, "People should not break God's laws."

"Sarah, that is the answer that most people would give. They think that as long as they don't hurt someone that they have not sinned. (+)

"Grandpa, can you give me an example where a sin of omission is worse than a sin of commission?" asked Tim.

"Yes," answered Grandpa, "but before we do, take this sheet of paper and draw a line down the middle of the page. On one side of the line write **commission** and on the other side write **omission**. I will do the same." Grandpa then proceeded to hand each of the two a sheet of paper."Tim, give me the first sin and I will write it down on my list."

The Sins of Commission	The Sins of Omission
Lying	Not praying
Stealing	Not witnessing
Cheating	Not studying God's Word
Swearing	Not being thankful to God
Killing	Not being thankful to parents
Adultery	Not giving to God
Fornication	Not showing kindness to the poor
Doing Drugs	Not helping people who are seeking
Disobeying parents	Not praying for your family
Getting Drunk	Not praying for sinners

"Now, that is ten on each side of our list, you get the idea." stated Grandpa. "Let me ask you according to Jesus which is the first or greatest commandment? Tim turn to Matthew 22:37 – 38 and read it for us. Then tell us what the greatest commandment is."

Matthew 22:37-38 – "Jesus said unto him, Thou shalt love the Lord thy God with **all thy heart**, and with **all thy soul**, and with **all thy mind**. This is the **first and great commandment**."

But often times the sins of omission which people fail to do are worse than the sins they commit."

116

"Love God with all your heart and with all of your soul and with all of your mind came the answer." (+)

"Is that a command, Tim?" asked Grandpa.

"In verse 37, Jesus said it was a commandment, Grandpa," answered Sarah.

"So if a person doesn't obey that commandment he has committed a sin of...." Grandpa paused in order for the children to finish the sentence.

They both answer, "COMMISSION."

"But it is also a sin which is generally committed as a sin of **omission** ." again Grandpa waited for them to respond.

"OMISSION"

"So this commandment to love God with all of your heart, all of your soul and all of your mind should go on what side of our line?"

Sarah and Tim both answered, "Both sides."

"Yet, we do not have it written down on either side, and Jesus said it was the **first or greatest commandment**"

Both of the young people just sat there as if to say, "what is the answer, Grandpa?" What people call bad sins and what God calls bad wins are quite different." God said, in ISAIAH 5:20 – *Woe unto them that call evil good, and good evil; that put darkness for light, and light for darkness; that put bitter for sweet, and sweet for bitter!*

Many times in God's eyes the sins of omission are much worse than the sin of commission, like murder or stealing.

"God gives people life and blesses them both materially and spiritually, but they commit **a horrible sin of omission.**"

"What is that sin of omission, Grandpa?" inquired Sarah.

"Sarah, let's ask God to answer that question."

"Can a maid forget her ornaments (jewelry – rings) or a bride her attire (wedding dress)? Yet my people have **forgotten me days without number**. Jeremiah 2:32 Throughout the history of Israel the Jewish people would become slothful in their religious services and then a few years later they would turn away from following the principles of God. In Hosea 8:14 we have the final, drastic conclusion. God reports, "**For Israel hath forgotten his maker**, and buildeth temples (where they would have formal dead services and adopt false religion). This would lead to their descendants embracing a false plan of salvation and dying lost, still in their sins."

"It all started through the sins of omission."

GOD'S CONDEMNATION ON THE
SIN OF OMISSION.

Fathers are to teach, train, love and supply the needs while protecting their wife and children. (+) Men through their **self-centeredness commits sins of omission** and do not take care of their family.

God sees the hurt and destruction that the sin of omission causes and sternly rebukes. His words are; "If a father does not take care of his family he denies the faith (truths of the Bible) and is WORSE THAN AN INFIDEL." (+) An infidel is the worse kind of sinner. I Tim 5:8

The reason God is so direct in his condemnation is – the man claims to be a Christian-- He neglects and abuses his family, which the unsaved observe and see. This causes them to turn away from Christ and salvation.

The man's family suffers from the sin of omission. **Instead of being loved they are neglected (or worse).** Instead of being trained they are taught horrible hurtful lessons that kill their self-confidence. Through their dad's neglect—they received a distorted view of God and turned away from Him to a wasted life, and finally an eternity in hell.

WHY THIS LESSON ON THE SIN OF OMISSION?

"Grandpa, I've become more conscious of how God looks at sin,"

God sees the hurt and destruction that the sin of omission causes and sternly rebukes. His words are; 'If a father does not take care of his family he denies the faith (truths of the Bible) and is WORSE THAN AN INFIDEL. (+) An infidel is the worse kind of sinner. I Tim 5:8

119

commented Sarah. "but what does this have to do with today's lesson?"

"Good question, Sarah. I was just coming to that." "FORGIVE US OUR DEBTS AS WE FORGIVE OUR DEBTORS" is our study today. I have tried to show you how that through **the sin of omission much harm is caused.**"

"WE OWE GOD our love but many times we don't pay it."

"We owe him **our gratitude, our praise, our faithful service**—many times we offend him by not paying our debts to him."

"We owe our children, our parents, our fellow man debts which we do not pay. Jesus taught us in the model prayer to face the debts and to forgive people who have failed or offended us, because we offend or fail Him much more than anyone ever hurts or fails us."

When the apostles were taught this principle they asked, "How often should we forgive, 'til seven times? Jesus answered their question by saying, 'til seventy times seven' (or an unlimited number of times).

The reason for this unlimited mercy and forgiveness is to keep us healthy spiritually. (+) Unforgiveness soon turns into bitterness, which not only destroys the one with bitterness, but the family and friends around the person who has bitterness. It also causes the person to fail to fulfill his purpose on earth. He soon manifests a bad attitude (non-Christian) which turns people away from Christ to remain in their sins forever.

WHEN WE PRAY

We ask God to forgive us our debts or sins. He has taught us to forgive others of their debts toward us.

Our parents owed us the obligation or debt to be there for us when we needed them. They did not pay that debt. We are to forgive them for not fulfilling their duty or debt toward us as God has forgiven us our failures.

We are to forgive those who have wronged us as God has forgiven us for wronging him, for not fulfilling our duties toward him.(+)

If we obey this simple command of forgiving others who have wronged us or who have let us down and were not there when we needed them, **then we keep a clean heart**. We keep the fellowship with our heavenly Father intact. We rejoice at his presence and blessings. We safeguard our hearts so there is no unforgiveness there. We have forgiven the insult. We have forgiven them for breaking a promise. We have forgiven the debt, which they owed us.

> "We owe our children, our parents, our fellow man debts which we do not pay. Jesus taught us in the model prayer to face the debts and to forgive people who have failed or offended us because we offend or fail Him much more than anyone ever hurts or fails us."

By praying and practicing this great principle of "forgiving those who trespass against us as God has forgiven us our trespasses," we remain a happy fruitful Christian.

SARAH'S SAD EXAMPLE

"What's the matter Sarah?" inquired Grandpa, "you look so sad."

"I'm sorry, Grandpa, what you taught about forgiveness explains what happened last year to my best friend, Beth."

"Yes, I meant to ask you about her. You were always together but I haven't seen her in ages," answered Grandpa.

> Our parents owed us the obligation or debt to be there for us when we needed them. They did not pay that debt. We are to forgive them for not fulfilling their duty or debt toward us as God has forgiven us our failures.

"She got offended at what happened at school. Some kids were saying things about her that were not true. She began to argue with them. She vowed she would get even with them, and that became all she talked about. I tried to get her to forget it. I told her that no one believed it, but she wouldn't listen. She began to change, and now she is cold and withdrawn toward everyone.(+)"

"She sure is," confirmed Tim

"It really hurts me," Sarah continued as she choked back the tears. "I really miss her."

"That's a perfect illustration Sarah, of what Jesus was warning the disciples. Unforgiveness is a very deadly sin which dries up and changes people. Let me point out another Bible truth. God promises to work all things together for good to those that love him. Sarah, it is obvious by the life you live that you love the Lord. It is also very clear that unforgiveness is destroying your friend, both of which is bad."

"God is working out that hurtful experience to your good by teaching you to always be very mindful to forgive and keep a sweet spirit."

"You see the terrible harm it causes the person who does not forgive. In this way God can make a bad experience work out to the good of those who love God. Praying this model prayer every day is a good dose of preventative medicine—it will keep us healthy."

Forgive us our debts as we forgive our debtors should be utmost in our thoughts as we live a happy life of service to our Savior.

POINTS TO PONDER

❖ We are commanded to love God with all our HEART, SOUL and MIND.

❖ The sin of omission is what brought destruction to Israel.

❖ Bitterness is more deadly than cancer.

❖ Forgiveness is preventative medicine.

❖ Bitterness will not break our relationship with God, but it will destroy our fellowship with Him.

Lesson Eight

After this manner therefore pray ye: Our Father which art in heaven, Hallowed be thy name. Thy kingdom come. Thy will be done in earth, as [it is] in heaven. Give us this day our daily bread. And forgive us our debts, as we forgive our debtors. AND LEAD US NOT INTO TEMPTATION, BUT DELIVER US FROM EVIL: For thine is the kingdom, and the power, and the glory, forever. AMEN. Matthew. 6:9-13

ADDITIONAL SCRIPTURE REFERENCE:
MATTHEW 6:6-15
Luke 5:5-13

Lesson Eight
LEAD US NOT INTO TEMPTATION, BUT DELIVER US FROM EVIL

"Hi, kids, are you ready for another lesson?" greeted Grandpa as his two students seated themselves.

"We came hungry," responded Tim.
Grandpa looked up with a questioning look on his face.

"For spiritual food," continued Sarah. All three enjoyed a good laugh at the kid's attempted humor.

PREVENTIVE MEDICINE LEADS US NOT INTO TEMPTATION BUT DELIVERS US FROM EVIL

"People are like the young man who confessed as he sat down at a huge banquet, "**I can resist everything except temptation.**" That is exactly the lesson that Jesus taught the apostles to pray, "**Lead us not into temptation but deliver us from evil.**" Man has a very, very hard time resisting temptation. (+)

"Adam and Eve sure proved that point, didn't they Grandpa?" committed Tim.

"Why is it so hard to resist temptation?," Sarah asked.

"Let us get into our lesson and see," answered Grandpa.

LEAD US NOT INTO TEMPTATION, WHY?

ONE SHOULD PRAY THAT PRAYER EVERY DAY IN ORDER TO OFFSET MAN'S GREATEST TENDENCY—TO WALK IN HIS OWN STRENGTH.

"A baby Christian starts out his Christian life with fear and trembling. (+) He prays, he repents, he goes to the alter for rededication and with much fear and trembling grows as a Christian. After a period of time something happens. He gets into the hang of living the Christian life. He learns the talk and imitates the Christian walk. He loses some of the fear and trembling. He comes to the conclusion that I can handle it— living this Christian Life" (+) So he begins to live a carnal, worldly life and falls into sin.

"Is that the reason that Paul pleaded with the members of the Roman Church to present their bodies as a living sacrifice, holy, acceptable unto God,?" asked Tim.

"Yes, answered Grandpa. Look in Romans 12:3 and see the reason Paul warned them. "That every man THINK NOT MORE HIGHLY OF HIMSELF (HIS ABILITIES) THAN HE OUGHT TO THINK," (+) (or/become confident in his own ability.)

In Paul's letter to the Corinthian church he recounts several experiences that the nation of Israel had which brought them heartache and judgment. After giving these examples against self sufficiency, he made this warning, "WHEREFORE, LET HIM THAT

THINKETH HE STANDETH TAKE HEED, LEST HE FALL (I Corinthians. 10:12)."

Lead us not into temptation, why? Because, in our own human strength we cannot withstand temptation and sin. (+) We are actually walking in sin (pride) which is one of the most destructive sins. How can we withstand sin when we are walking in the sin of pride?

LEAD US NOT INTO TEMPTATION, WHY? IN ORDER TO KEEP MAN FROM MAKING HIS WORST CALCULATION

"Most people do not understand the two-fold nature of a Christian."

"When a person was born into the human family he received a depraved, sinful, lustful nature that unless it is restrained, is capable of any sin." (+) When that same person is born again into God's family, he receives a divine, holy nature. **That gives him two natures.**

The Bible talks **of the Spirit and the flesh,** the new and old man; and the inward and outward man. (+) These natures are the exact opposite and war against each other; both want to be boss in the believer's life.

What do these have in common?
"Resist the devil and he will flee from you"
"WHEN YE PRAY SAY"
"Abstain from, all appearance of evil"
They are all commandments of God!

When a person is born again and becomes active in serving the Lord, he feeds the inward man who grows in strength and controls the flesh, and the Christian lives a holy life. While he is feeding the spiritual man, he is also starving the fleshly man. (+) But although he is starving the fleshly man, it is still very much alive, and if given a chance, will fight the spiritual man for control of the believer's life again.

As the new Christian enjoys his new found spiritual life, HE MISCALCULATES WHY HE IS ABLE TO LIVE A GOOD, HAPPY, SPIRITUAL LIFE. (+) The new Christian deducts, "I have changed." I am not the same man I was before I became a Christian, but he is. He has the same flesh nature and if he gets his eyes on himself and calculates that he is a strong Christian who can resist temptation, he will soon fall into sin. When this happens to a child of God his prayers soon go unanswered and he becomes a nominal Christian.

"He doesn't realize that he is strong because he has been feeding the spiritual man while starving the fleshly man, isn't that right Grandpa?" asked Tim.

"Yes, that is correct, Tim," commented Grandpa…when **he begins to take credit for his spiritual growth** that very act starts feeding the fleshly man." PRIDE IS A FOOD FOR THE FLESHLY MAN. SELF-SUFFICIENCY IS A FOOD FOR THE FLESHLY MAN. (+) Believing that he can go places where there is temptation to the fleshly man is food for the fleshly nature. As he feeds the fleshly nature pride and self-sufficiency he weakens the spiritual man and will soon make shipwreck of his life unless he repents.

"Grandpa, praying everyday, - **Lead us not into temptation but deliver us from evil**, would help prevent that, wouldn't it?" asked Sarah.

"That is the reason Jesus taught them to pray that way, Sarah."

TO GET OUT OF THE WILL OF GOD IS TO SELF-DESTRUCT

King David got out of God's will by staying home WHEN IT WAS TIME FOR KINGS TO GO TO WAR. When one is out of the will of God he has no protection against temptation.(+)

> **David looked.**
> **David lusted.**
> **David gave into temptation.**
> **David had a one-night stand and still bears the scars today!**

God could save David from the bear. He could save David from the lion. He could save David from the giant and a thousand other dangers, but he could not save **David from himself** when David became self-sufficient and started walking in the flesh. (+) Lead us not into temptation but deliver us from evil will save the Christian from his WORST CALCULATIONS, SELF SUFFICIENCY.

"Who was the wisest man of his day, Tim?" asked Grandpa?

"Solomon," came a ready answer.

Solomon trusted in his own wisdom and made shipwreck of his life, his family's lives and divided his kingdom. (+)

"Grandpa, you named it!" "What a disaster!" exclaimed Sarah.

"Who was the strongest man in the Bible, Sarah?" came a question from Grandpa.

"That's easy, Sampson," was her reply.

"When Sampson began to walk in his own strength what happened to him?"

"His enemies plucked out his eyes and he became a blind slave," Sarah answered.

"They humiliated him by making him do the work of a beast while they taunted him," continued Tim.

NOT BY MIGHT OR BY POWER

"Kids, think that through. What is the lesson God is trying to tell his children?"

"Was the brilliant mental power of Solomon able to deliver him from temptation?" continued Grandpa.

God could save David from the bear. He could save David from the lion. He could save David from the giant and a thousand other dangers, but he could not save **David from himself** when David became self-sufficient and started walking in the flesh.

131

"No!" came the answer from both young people.

"The very opposite is true. It was Solomon's self assurance which got him into trouble."

"Was the might or strength of Sampson able to deliver him from temptation?"

"No!" came the resounding reply.

"But both of these men, Solomon and Sampson started out as humble dedicated servants of the Lord with the blessings of God upon their lives." (+) "Little by little they forsook God's grace and leadership until the temptation they faced CAUSED BOTH OF THEIR DEATH'S PREMATURELY."

Long ago the prophet stated that the only way his people would be delivered from the temptation which would lead to evil (destruction). **He said**, "it is not by might (physical strength) it is not by power (mental ability) but it is by my Spirit saith the Lord." **(+)**

LEAD US NOT INTO TEMPTATION, WHY?
IT IS THE ONLY SAFE PATH TO WALK IN

The book of Proverbs is God's book for parents. It clearly gives the principles for the discipling of their children. It clearly gives the children instruction of behavior toward their parents and how to grow into a happy and successful Christian adult.

In this book of wisdom and instruction we find this strong teaching to guard against and overcome temptation. "ENTER NOT INTO THE PATH OF THE WICKED (Proverbs 4:14). This is pretty clear, isn't it Tim?"

"Yes sir," came Tim's response.

"Sarah, look at the double stating of that same principle. Read it for Grandpa."

Sarah read, **"And go not in the way of the wicked men."** There must be a real danger in exposing oneself to temptation for God to repeat it.

"Read the next two words and stop, Tim."

"Avoid it."

"Avoid what, Tim."

"The paths of wicked men, Grandpa," came Tim's humble reply.

Sarah, read the next four words for Grandpa. **"PASS NOT BY IT,"**.

"Pass not by what, Sarah?"

"The path of wicked men, Sir."

"How would you do that, Sarah?"

"Well, you would detour around it or turn around and go another way," she answered.

"That's good, Sarah!"

Turning to Tim he said, "Read the next three words for me, please."

"Turn from it," read Tim.   "That means the same thing Sarah said", commented Tim.

"Look at the last three words in this verse: "and **pass away**." LITERALLY RUN AWAY. (+)   "Do as Joseph did who fled from Potipher's wife. Run for your life—get away from temptation."

"Look at the complete statement in verse fifteen which teaches us how to resist temptation and evil: **avoid it, pass not by it, turn from it, and pass away (run away or flee)."** (+)

"Now kids, let us all read the following verse to see the reason for this wise council. "For they (the evil people) SLEEP NOT, EXCEPT THEY HAVE DONE MISCHIEF; AND

> **Go not in the way of the wicked man.**
> **Avoid it.**
> **Pass not by it.**
> **Turn from it.**
> **Pass away (run away from it).**

THEIR SLEEP IS TAKEN AWAY (THEY CAN'T SLEEP) UNLESS THEY CAUSE SOME TO FALL." (+)   This verse reveals that when one begins to flirt with things that don't seem too bad, he is deceived.   Behind the bright lights, the inviting music and the gay laughter **lies evil, addicting people WHO WANT TO DESTROY YOU."** (+)

"God knows the weakness of our flesh.   God knows the evil traps that wicked people set. Evil people dress up the event and make it look innocent and oh, so much fun."

"God knows the addicting nature of the flesh, therefore he tells us the only safe path for his children to walk in are the paths that are lighted as we do his will. **Walk in the safe light of his Holy Word**.

When one exposes the flesh to temptation He will find that he can resist **everything except temptation**. The safe and only way in resisting temptation is to obey God's command in daily prayer. LEAD US NOT INTO TEMPTATION BUT DELIVER US FROM EVIL.

DELIVER US FROM EVIL

"Tim, would you take a gun and deliberately blow someone's head off?" asked Grandpa.

"That's gross, Grandpa," commented Sarah in horror.

"No," came Tim's startled reply.

"Why?" asked Grandpa?

"That would be murder," answered Tim.

"And murder is a very wicked sin, or could be a very evil sin, isn't that right?" added Grandpa.

"That is right, sir," replied Tim.

"Grandpa, what is the difference between wicked and evil?" asked Sarah.

"Sarah, an evil sin is something more deliberate and sinister than a wicked sin. An evil intent is to do one more hurt and harm than something that is done by a wicked person."

"I asked Tim that startling question in order to shock him and make him think," continued Grandpa.

"It sure did that," Tim said.

"Your question sure caught me by surprise," confessed Sarah.

"Sarah, that is exactly what sin does," added Grandpa. "It catches people completely off guard. Something that they didn't think was very bad suddenly mushrooms into a major hurt, or even a crime."

"The process of a problem is first, a temptation. The person understands that it is wrong but the act seems harmless." (+)

"That harmless thought or act suddenly takes on a new role. It becomes a sin. The sin becomes more than one issue; it becomes more complicated as one tries to justify or cover up their indiscretions. As they do so the sin takes a turn for the worse and becomes wickedness. Wickedness complicates the problems and the situation grows into something that causes the person to do an evil act. David, who gave in to temptation and had an affair with Bathsheba, is a perfect example of what I am saying lead us not into temptation.

LEAD US NOT INTO TEMPTATION KEEPS US FROM EVIL

If a child of God could understand the horrible consequences of yielding to temptation he would heed God's commands of : (+)

Go not in the way of the wicked man.
Avoid it.
Pass not by it.
Turn from it.
Pass away (run away from it).

God knows the horrible outcome of yielding to temptation, so he placed it in the model prayer so his children would be reminded of sin's deadly consequences. (+)

Lead us not into temptation but deliver us from evil is a phrase that his children should pray every day. (+) It is our Father's way of turning us away from wickedness and evil. It is his way of making us alert to the potential destruction that hides behind the door of temptation. (everyday)

PEOPLE GIVE INTO TEMPTATION BECAUSE THEY DON'T SEE THE SINFULNESS OF SIN

It was only a "little white lie!," "No," it was breaking one of God's 10 commandments, which commanded that "thou shalt not bear false witness." When one breaks one of God's commandments **he is sinning** by disobeying God. When one dishonors his father and mother he not only disobeys his parents, but **he sins against God** by breaking one of his laws. (+)

Taking God's name in vain is a direct offense against the one who gives you life. God gives you life, redeems you from hell by dying in your place and gives hundreds of blessings including the one of breath, which one uses to take God's name in vain.   WHAT WICKEDNESS!

When one understands that in the law dispensation, people were stoned to death for breaking one of the 10 commandments, they would see the sinfulness of sin.

Grandpa concludes his class by saying, "Let us not take the expression, **lead us not into temptation but deliver us from evil LIGHTLY.**" It is God's red flag **indicating danger and potential destruction. (+)**

"What a wise and gracious Lord," commented Tim.

"**What a wise and gracious Father** is the spirit of the model prayer, isn't it Grandpa?" asked Sarah.

"Yes, Sarah, it is."   "Let us close our lesson today by praying together," he paused; and the children joined him in praying: LEAD US NOT INTO TEMPTATION, BUT DELIVER US FROM EVIL.

POINTS TO PONDER

- Man's greatest tendency is to walk in his own strength.

- The tendency to walk in his own strength DESTROYED SAMPSON.

- MAN CAN RESIST EVERYTHING EXCEPT TEMPTATION.

- The only way a person can resist temptation is:
    - Go not in the way of the wicked man
    - Avoid it
    - Pass not by it
    - Turn from it
    - Pass away (run away from it)

- A simple temptation led TO KING DAVID COMMITTING MUCH EVIL.

Lesson Nine

AFTER THIS MANNER THEREFORE PRAY YE: Our Father which art in heaven, Hallowed be thy name. Thy kingdom come. Thy will be done in earth, as [it is] in heaven. Give us this day our daily bread. And forgive us our debts, as we forgive our debtors. And lead us not into temptation, but deliver us from evil: FOR THINE IS THE KINGDOM, and the power, and the glory, forever.
AMEN.

Matthew 6:9-13

LESSON NINE
FOR THINE IS THE KINGDOM

"Good afternoon kids. What do you have there?" inquired Grandpa.

"Some chocolate chip cookies," replied Sarah.

"Sarah baked them especially for her teacher," informed Tim.

"Great! I can hardly believe how you kids are growing up. I am so proud of you. Set them right over there and we will enjoy them together after our lesson."

"Tim, have you ever stopped and counted the number of words in the model prayer?" asked Grandpa.

"No sir," responded Tim.

"Me neither, Grandpa," volunteered Sarah.

"How many books are there in the Bible?"

Both children responded at the same time, "**sixty-six**."

"That is right, and there are **sixty-six words in the model prayer also**," informed Grandpa. That is a very short prayer isn't it?"

"In this short prayer of only sixty-six words we have 'THE KINGDOM' MENTIONED TWICE, which means that a proper understanding of the kingdom is very important." (+)

EVERYTHING BELONGS TO GOD

Jesus commanded the apostles to pray every day **"Thine is the Kingdom,"** which reinforces that God is the supreme ruler of the earth and is in control of everything! (+)

IT ALL BELONGS TO HIM

One of the first major lessons that God wanted to establish early in the history of mankind, was that He was the supreme king of the earth. He inspired the prophet Daniel to write a history of the

> "In this short prayer of only sixty-six words we have 'THE KINGDOM' MENTIONED TWICE, which means that a proper understanding of the kingdom is very important."

major powers of the world hundreds of years before those nations became world powers.(+)

In the book of Daniel he lists the succession of the four ruling nations of Babylon; the Medes and Persians followed by Greece and finally, the Roman Empire (Daniel 7:27).

"Bear in mind kids, that the book of Daniel was written in the sixth century before the birth of Christ."
"Sixth century before the birth of Jesus?" puzzled Sarah.

"That is six hundred years before Jesus was born, right Grandpa," explained Tim.

"Yes, but the important point I wish to make, kids, concerning the book of Daniel is the following statement. Read Daniel 2:44 for us Tim."

Tim read, "And in the days of these kings shall the God of heaven set up a kingdom, which shall never be destroyed: and the kingdom shall not be left to other people, but it shall break in pieces and consume all these kingdoms, and **it shall stand for ever.**" (+)

"In Daniel 4:17 the Bible declares 'that the -most high (God) ruleth in the kingdom of men.' When Nebuchadnezzar failed to recognize the supremacy of God's power, God caused the king to loose his mind for seven years. He lived like an animal and grew feathers like a bird. When God turned Nebuchadnezzar's sanity back then the king spoke a truth that the whole world should know. He said, speaking of God, **"whose Dominion is an everlasting dominion and his kingdom is from generation to generation (Dan. 4:34).**" (+)

PHARAOH INSULTED GOD

"In Exodus chapter five, Pharaoh insulted and challenged God by saying, "I know not the Lord and neither will I let Israel go" —**Egypt was the world power when Pharaoh challenged God.** When the combat was over Pharaoh was dead and his nation was in shambles. God had demonstrated that he is in charge of the whole earth."

GOLIATH CURSED, CHALLENGED AND INSULTED GOD

"For forty days a huge giant cursed, challenged and insulted God and his chosen people, Israel. God sent an unarmed teenage boy out against him, and the world has marveled at the **story of David slaying Goliath ever since.**"

"Solomon stated that the king's heart was in the hand of God and that he turneth it whatsoever way he wants."

"In Proverbs 8:15, the Bible clearly states, that God is the supreme ruler of the earth. "By me kings reign, and princes decree justice." "By me princes rule and nobles, even all judges of the earth." They all rule by God's permissive will. Many of them are very wicked rulers and do the opposite of what God's will is. They may even persecute God's people. "In the sixth chapter of Revelation, the antichrist came upon the earth to do his dirty work by God's permissive will."

Soon God will crush all these evil rulers and put the antichrist (devil) down into hell, and establish his glorious, peaceful, one thousand year reign of righteousness. He commanded the apostles to constantly reaffirm his power by praying, **"Thine is the kingdom."**

> **What do these have in common?**
> "Whether ye eat or drink do all to the glory of God"
> "WHEN YE PRAY SAY"
> "Preach the Word"
>
> **They are all commandments of God!**

THINE IS THE KINGDOM; IT IS ALL OVERSEEN BY HIM

"From the massive galaxies which travel at the same speed, and are in perfect harmony with each other, although they may be a million light years apart to the smallest hair that falls aimlessly from a head; **God controls it all." (+)**

"All of the billions of stars sing unto the creator, and he knows each one of them by name. There is not a little bird that falls that escapes God's all seeing eye (Matthew 6).

"There is not a word spoken but what God does hear and record" (Psalm 139:4). "Nothing is covered by darkness because the 'darkness and the light are both alike to Thee (God)" (Psalm 139:12).

"All hairs of one's head are numbered. "How precious also are thy thoughts unto me, O God! How great is the sum of them (Ps. 139:17).' (+) There are so many that the number of God's thoughts, toward his children, cannot be numbered. Verse eighteen states that his thoughts are more in number than the sand."

"Paul gave an announcement which applies to every human being when he stated, "In him, we live, move, and have our being" (Acts 17)." (+)

"God commanded the apostles to pray every day, THINE IS THE KINGDOM because every thing is overseen by him and under his watchful eye."

SOME PRACTICAL BENEFITS OF PRAYING, THINE IS THE KINGDOM

"Kids, can you see how important this part of The Model Prayer is?"

The children just sat and pondered his question as he continued to explain.

"When sickness and death invades the home and things are lonely and black – praying, 'Thine is the Kingdom' reminds them that God is still in charge and that the 'Father is there'."

"That is wonderful, isn't it Grandpa," stated Sarah.

When there is trouble in life, harsh words and great disappointments, praying, "Thine is the Kingdom," reassures that the "Father is there" and he has promised never to leave or forsake us.

The Devil gets in a church and misunderstandings cause great heartache and sorrow! Praying "Thine is the Kingdom" causes faith to go on.

THE MANAGEMENT OF THE KINGDOM

"When the apostles prayed, '**Thy kingdom come**' everyday, they

---

Twenty-Third Psalm
(Vest-Pocket Edition)

Beneath me: Green pastures;
Beside me :Still waters;
With me: my Shepherd;
Before me :a table;
Around me: mine enemies;
After me: goodness and mercy;
Beyond me: the house of the Lord

had the future millennial kingdom reinforced in their thinking. (+) By praying, '**thine is the kingdom**' which acknowledged God's great power and purpose, it caused them to live in expectancy of Christ's coming soon. In other words, Tim, the coming kingdom in the apostles thinking was drawing near, just like summer is drawing near to you."

"Now Tim, when school is over and summer vacation begins what is on your agenda?"

"A job, my first real job, Grandpa, and you are right; I'm really looking forward to it," answered Tim.

"Tim, I can feel the excitement in your voice," replied Grandpa.

"Grandpa, why did you change the subject? I was really interested in the apostles and the coming kingdom," scolded Sarah.

"I didn't change the subject, Sarah, **I am illustrating the subject**. After the 40 days of teaching which Jesus (Acts 1:3) gave the apostles, they were totally excited about their new jobs **on the management team under King Jesus in the millennial**." (+)

In Daniel, Chapter seven, it reveals the end of the Anti – Christ's short reign on this earth. Then in verse 27 it talks about the greatness of the millennial Kingdom UNDER THE WHOLE HEAVEN.

"Now kids, read the rest of the verse. It is like a sign advertising... *HELP WANTED*. The verse states, 'Kingdom under whole heaven shall be given to the people of the Saints of the most high, whose kingdom is an everlasting kingdom and all dominions shall serve and obey him.' Note the help wanted sign is directed to **the people (all ages) of the saints**."

HELP WANTED SIGN

"Tim, since I am teaching you and Sarah how and why you should pray, **I am going to use the sign for employment which got your attention** and caused you to make application for the job."

"What were the three things which first grabbed your attention?"

"Well, **the company that was hiring really got my attention,**" replied Tim.

"**It is a Fortune 500 Company**, Grandpa, volunteered Sarah, that has **facilities all over the world**."

"And, what else, Tim" asked Grandpa?

"**They were looking for people of character** whom they would train to fill top managerial positions. (+) They even start training sixteen year olds who are still in high school."

"Anything else, Tim?" Grandpa continued.

"**The pay!**" gleefully shouted Sarah.

"Yes, they have a surprising compensational package with many benefits," (+) considered Tim.

"Were there any special qualifications or tests given in order to qualify, Tim?"

"Were there? Boy, did I have to study! And there was a time or two in which I didn't think I would make it."

"Grandpa, Sarah interrupted, What does all this have to do with prayer or the kingdom?"

"Sarah, I know that you and Tim, along with the whole family, have been involved with Tim's application, tests, and success of being hired by the company. **I would like to take this physical effort of getting a secular job and apply it to obtaining a position in a spiritual company.** As I studied Daniel 7:27 I was impressed by the statements, 'shall be given to the people of the saints.' It is like a job wanted sign, designed to attract workers for the kingdom." (+)

"You kids can help me construct a **help wanted sign for workers in the coming kingdom**."

"What would be the first thing we would do?" asked Grandpa?

"Give notice that the company is hiring?" suggested Sarah.

"How would you do that?" continued Grandpa.

"By building a help wanted sign and making it visible to the whole country, she continued."

"Okay, we have a large *HELP WANTED* sign. Now what should we place on the sign?"

"You would focus on the people you are trying to attract for the positions, Sarah said, as she remembered the huge sign which was posted outside Tim's new employer."

"**Management Positions are now open to all Ages,**" stated Grandpa. (+)

"Next you would tell them about the company who is seeking employees," offered Sarah.

"No, that came last on the sign, corrected Tim. The next statement which was in large red letters was GOOD ASSOCIATES."

"Oh yeah, admitted Sarah, the words under good associates, but in smaller letters were wonderful working conditions." (+) Then came the statement, **good, vested secure positions.** Vested means that you can earn benefits that cannot be lost, Sarah offered."

"Dad had to tell you that," Tim said.

"That's right, but I still remember, defended Sarah."

"Then, at the bottom of the sign came the name of the company in big bold letters Tim said."

"Yes, answered Sarah, one side of the sign was, *Now Hiring*".

"On the other side of the sign was the statement, *Candidates Will Be Tested*, said Tim. I will never forget that."

"Okay, said Grandpa grabbing a clipboard, let's construct a sign for the upcoming kingdom, as he begins to write."

H-E-L-P   W-A-N-T-E-D

GOOD ASSOCIATES
All in glorified bodies

WONDERFUL WORKING CONDITIONS
Peace on earth – Good will toward men. (+)

SECURED VESTED POSITION
Appointed by Jesus for 1000 years.

THE KINGDOM OF OUR LORD SOLE PROPRIETOR
Jesus is King of Kings and Lord of Lords.

NOW HIRING
CANDIDATES WILL BE TRIED AND TESTED

"Wow, Grandpa, are there really managerial positions open in the coming Kingdom, asked Tim?" "What kind of test will we have to take?....."

"Are there ads in the Bible that state that God is now hiring, interrupted Sarah?"

"Yes, replied Grandpa, but let's take those questions one at a time. In answering your first question concerning managerial positions which shall be open in the Millennial Kingdom, please note Matthew19:28 which teaches that the twelve apostles were offered

managerial positions of being kings over the twelve
tribes of Israel." (+)

"Luke quoted the Lord of the faithful servants, concerning the managerial positions that he promised them, as '**mayors or governors over ten cities while others would supervise or manage five cities.'** " **(Luke 19: 16-19)**

Occupation Unchanged

An infidel was introduced by a gentleman to a minister with a remark, "He never attends public worship." "Ah!" said the minister, "I hope you are mistaken." "By no means," said the stranger; "I always spend Sunday in settling my accounts." "Then, alas," was the calm but solemn reply, "you will find, sir, that the day of judgment will be spent in the same manner."

"**Some will rule over whole nations.** (Rev. 2:26-27) Some will be lifted to the lofty managerial position **of sitting on the throne with King Jesus.**" (Revelation 3:20)

"Sarah, there is a story recorded in Matthew 19:27-30 through Matthew 20: 1-16 of the Lord of the Harvest **hiring workers...**"

"Really, Grandpa, does it really use the word **hire**?"

"Really," laughed Grandpa, he not only hired them but in the story he pays the workers."

"The story begins by the Lord of the vineyard hiring workers at 6:00 in the morning **for a darius or a day's pay**. The workers are to reap the grapes who represent lost people. At nine o' clock in the morning he hires additional workers. He hires more workers at 12:00

152

noon and hires additional workers at the 9th hour (3:00 o'clock)."

"At the eleventh hour (5:00 p.m.) He finds other workers standing idle and asks them the question, '**why stand ye here all the day idle?**'"

"Their answer to his question Sarah was, **because no man hath HIRED US.**" (+)

"Really," responded Sarah.

"The Lord of the harvest told them, "**go ye also into the vineyard and whatever is right, that shall you receive.**"

"Sarah, the most surprising thing is not that he hired them to work the final hour of the day but HE PAID THE WORKERS HIRED LAST, FIRST. The ones who had worked all day were paid last."

Tim said, "Grandpa is that really in the Bible?"

"What does that story mean, asked Sarah?"

"The day from 6 a.m. to 6 p.m. represents **the whole church or grace dispensation from the time of the apostles to the end of the age when Jesus comes back.**"

"THE ELEVENTH HOUR STANDS FOR THE PERIOD OF TIME right before the close of the age." (+)

"The vineyard represent THE SIX AND A HALF BILLION PLUS PEOPLE who are alive in the world today."

"The workers that he hires in the eleventh hour are the Christians who are alive on the earth today and are the ones he is attempting to hire and work at winning souls in the vineyard today. (+)TIME IS RUNNING OUT IN THIS DISPENSATION, soon the sun will set on the massive harvest of six and half billion souls. Jesus died for every one of them and he is not willing that any of them perish, but he needs workers to go into the harvest and win them before time ends."

"The story teaches that anyone, regardless of their age or regardless of their past, will be paid just as much as if they had worked all their life for Him."

"Tim, you are seventeen years old, Sarah you are thirteen…"

"Almost fourteen, Grandpa."

"If Jesus should come in the next ten years, Tim, you would have barely started adult life. Sarah, you would be a young woman of only twenty-four years."

"But, if you kids really began to live for the Lord and majored on winning and discipling people, the Lord promises that he will pay or reward you as if you worked for him 40-50 years, or all of your life."

"That is a vivid story, Grandpa, and it challenges my heart," said Tim.

"Me too," echoed Sarah.

"But I always thought that a Christian should serve the Lord because he loves him and not for a reward."

"Yes, we discussed that point before didn't we kids."

LOVE IS THE SUPREME MOTIVE
FOR SERVICE

"Kids, let us turn to I Corinthians 13:1-3 and examine the supreme motive for serving the Lord. Verse one states that although one could speak with the languages of men and even of angels, and does not speak out of love (of Christ) **he is just a noise maker.**"

"If one had the gift of speaking God's words with clearness and power and did not have the love of God when he was doing it, or if one had all faith so he could do great miracles or move mountains and has not the LOVE OF GOD (he doesn't do it because he loves the Lord.) HE IS NOTHING."

"The first of the 10 commandments command one to **love God with all his heart, soul and might. (+)** But kids, if you love someone, you want to be near to them. You want to enjoy their company and do things for them. If you love God you want to obey and please Him."

"If one loves God he wants to be in His presence and fellowship with him so he will be a blessing to him. Paul

> If one loves God he wants to be in His presence and fellowship with him so he will be a blessing to him.

has puzzled many Bible students and scholars by his testimony in (Philippians 3:7-14)."

155

"Although he was an outstanding Christian Paul states that he counts all of his accomplishments and righteousness as nothing if he can only know Jesus better (8:8). Again Paul says in verse 10 that he wanted to know Jesus better; he wanted to experience with Jesus in suffering for him. Then, in verse 11, he states, 'by any means I might attain unto the (higher order) resurrection of the dead.' Then in verse 14 he said he is pressing for the prize... ALL OF HIS LANGUAGE SIMPLY MEANS THAT HE LOVES

> TIME IS RUNNING OUT IN THIS DISPENSATION, soon the sun will set on the massive harvest of six and half billion souls. Jesus died for every one of them and he is not willing that any of them perish, but he needs workers to go into the harvest and win them before time ends.

JESUS, WANTS TO BE CLOSE TO HIM WHEN HE LEAVES HIS LIFE OF SERVICE ON THIS EARTH.. He is teaching that the greatest reward that a person can receive in the millennium IS TO BE CLOSELY ASSOCIATED WITH JESUS ON A DAY-BY-DAY BASIS AS HE RULES THIS WORLD. (+) Paul is not trying to win any rewards or positions for himself but he knows what the greatest reward will be. **It will be in a position, which is very close to his Savior who is now, King Jesus."**

"In the book of Revelation John writes to the seven churches of Asia. Most of those churches were having trials or suffering severe persecution."

"Jesus writes a letter to each of those seven churches. He commends them for the things they are doing right, and rebukes the churches who are doing wrong."

"He rebukes the church at Ephesus for they had left their first love which is the love people have for Jesus that causes them to win souls. (Revelation 2:4) But in verse seven he commends the members **who have overcome the trials by faith** by promising them a close fellowship with him. They would eat of the tree of life in midst of paradise of God. **That is close to God's throne where they would see and serve God in a personal, daily way. (+)** What a great reward for those who denied themselves, took up their cross and faithfully followed Jesus. They put winning souls and pleasing their Savior first in their lives during their journey though a wicked world and

> In order to make them conscious that he was the Supreme boss of the earth with ALL POWER, HE COMMANDS THEM TO PRAY (EVERY DAY) – "THINE IS THE KINGDOM."

now are **rewarded as they live in his daily presence**. Although there are seven churches and Jesus makes precious promises to every group of over-comers, we will only note two more of them. Kids, let us examine the tender words that Jesus spoke to the over-comers in the church of Philadelphia."

"Him that overcometh will I make a pillar in the temple of my God and **he shall go no more out**:" (their reward is to be near to Jesus). The verse continues, "and I will write upon him the name of my God, and the name of the city of my God which is new Jerusalem which cometh down out of heaven from my God and I will write upon him my new name." (Revelation 3:12).

"This close fellowship is given to people who walked by faith even though they experience trouble, trials and pain **because they loved and served Jesus."** (+)

"To the saints that overcame by faith and served the Lord out of love in the Laodician Church, Jesus promises this great reward."

"To him that overcometh **will I grant to set with me on my throne,** even as I also overcome and am set down with my Father in his throne." (Revelation 3:21)

"Jesus offered great rewards to motivate his children to stay busy winning souls and living for him. If they do, then he will share his time with them in a close, loving fellowship in his kingdom."

In order to keep the apostles minds pointed toward that glorious day of his coming he commanded them to pray every day, THY KINGDOM COME."

In order to make them conscious that he was the Supreme boss of the earth with ALL POWER, HE COMMANDS THEM TO PRAY (EVERY DAY) – "THINE IS THE KINGDOM."

"As they faced the trials and hardships of their ministry - they needed the assurance that God was still in charge, that he would work 'all things together' for their good."

"There is one additional scripture which Dr. Luke, the Beloved Physician, gives that states both the **HOW AND THE WHY OF BEING NEAR TO JESUS FOR THE 1000-YEAR REIGN.**

"He states THE HOW in Luke 12:31. But seek ye first the **Kingdom of God** and all these things (blessings) shall be added unto you." (+)

"The following verse gives THE WHY of the closeness in the millennial reign. He (Jesus) quotes, "Fear not, little flock: FOR IT IS YOUR FATHERS GOOD PLEASURE to give you the Kingdom." God wants to have his obedient children near him for the whole 1000 years!"

"Before you leave I want to assign your homework for our next lesson," stated Grandpa.

"Grandpa, you sure are a slave driver," joked Sarah.

"What is our assignment, Grand-pop? Tim asked using his endearing term for his Grandfather."

"Your homework assignment is to look up and see how many times you can find the expression, 'The Spirit of the Lord came upon----."

"To him that overcometh **will I grant to set with me on my throne**, even as I also overcome and am set down with my Father in his throne." (Revelation 3:21)

"Oh, that will be easy," replied Tim.

"And fun," said Sarah, as she hugged her Grandfather good-bye.

"This lesson on **Thine is the Kingdom** has really increased my confidence, confessed Tim."

"Yes, and if you pray everyday, 'THINE IS THE KINGDOM', your spiritual growth and confidence in God is just beginning."

POINTS TO PONDER

- ❖ **My Sovereign Father KNOWS all things.**

- ❖ **My Sovereign Father CONTROLS all things.**

- ❖ **My Sovereign Father WANTS ME TO RULE AND REIGN with his Son during the Millennium.**

- ❖ **My Sovereign Father wants TO HIRE ME to work in the final harvest of 6 ½ billion souls.**

- ❖ **My Sovereign Father OFFERS ME FAVORITE STATUS for 1,000 years if I do his work in my life NOW.**

Lesson Ten

AFTER THIS MANNER THEREFORE PRAY YE: Our Father which art in heaven, Hallowed be thy name. Thy kingdom come. Thy will be done in earth, as [it is] in heaven. Give us this day our daily bread. And forgive us our debts, as we forgive our debtors. And lead us not into temptation, but deliver us from evil: FOR THINE is the kingdom, and THE POWER, and the glory, forever. Amen.
-Matthew. 6:9-13

LESSON TEN
THINE IS... THE POWER

"Hello kids, it is good to see you this afternoon."

The children responded and sat down ready for their next lesson. **"Our lesson today is on Thine is The Power,"** stated Grandpa.

"But Grandpa, we have already studied about God's power in several of our lessons", answered Sarah.

"Yes Sarah, but that was God exercising his power in creations, in the universe and on the earth. We studied about his power over the nations and in the affairs of men, showing that he was the supreme owner and controller of all things."(+)

"In our study about power we dealt with his supremacy in the physical and intellectually realm. God demonstrated his indescribable physical power in the feats of creation and guiding the operation of all things both in the universe and on earth; then, when he was challenged by the ruler of the earth we soon realized God's great power."

"Because the foolishness of God is wiser than men, and the weakness of God is stronger than men. Paul is not saying God is foolish or weak. He is showing the greatness of God's wisdom compared to man, and is saying that God's weakest is light years stronger than man's best."

THINE IS... THE SPIRITUAL POWER

"In our lesson today we are studying about a spiritual power which the Christian needs in serving the Lord. Kids, please note this statement from the book of Zechariah which says 'not by might (physical power) not by power (intellectual power) but by my Spirit (Spiritual Power) saith the Lord of hosts.'(+) (Zechariah 6:4)"

"Let us further identify that when Jesus commanded the apostles to pray, saying 'THINE IS KINGDOM AND THE POWER,' that he was referring to His power in the spiritual realm."(+) Tim, read what King David said in Psalms 62:11

Tim responds by reading, "God hath spoken once; twice have I heard this; THAT POWER BELONGETH TO GOD."

FINALLY, Paul said, "And be not drunk with wine, wherein is excess; but BE FILLED WITH THE SPIRIT." (Ephesians 5:18)(+)

"Sarah, turn to the book of Micah and see what that prophet said."

"Micah, Five verse eight," Sarah said as she started reading, "But truly I am FULL OF POWER BY THE SPIRIT of the Lord, and of judgment and of might, to declare, unto Jacob his transgressions and to Israel his sin."

"Now, I will quote a few statements from the Apostle Paul."

"FIRST, Paul said, be strong in the Lord and the POWER OF HIS MIGHT." (Ephesians 6:10)

"SECOND, for the weapons of our warfare are not carnal, but MIGHTY THROUGH GOD (+) (spiritual) to the pulling down of strongholds (II Corinthians 10:4)".

FINALLY, Paul said, "And be not drunk with wine, wherein is excess; but BE FILLED WITH THE SPIRIT." (Ephesians 5:18)(+)

ENDUED WITH POWER FROM ON HIGH

"In the great commission recorded in Luke 24:46-49 the last verse commands the apostles to tarry in Jerusalem.(+) The first part of the great commission recorded by Luke is in harmony with Matthew, Mark and John concerning the world wide commission. All four writers stress the urgent need to get the gospel to every creature in the world. The Apostles have been trained to lead this gigantic effort of world evangelism. The masses of the earth were lost with many of them dying without Christ. **But, Jesus tells them to wait! Don't Go! Tarry!**"

"Why Grandpa? Why did Jesus first command them to go and then command them to tarry or wait?" asked Sarah.(+)

"That is the point we are trying to make in this lesson... THINE IS THE POWER, Sarah."

"Sarah, read with me as we

What do these have in common?

"Be not drunk with wine, but be ye filled with the Spirit"
"WHEN YE PRAY SAY"
"Study to shew thyself approved unto God a workman"

They are all commandments of God!

165

examine verse 49. Jesus said, "and behold I send the promise of the Father upon you: but tarry ye in the city of Jerusalem, **until ye be endued with power from on high**."

"What is the promise of the father?" asked Tim.

"Tim, when John the Baptist came as the forerunner of Christ to prepare the way for the coming of Jesus, he preached that God had sent him to baptize with water (those that were saved), but the coming son of God would baptize with the Holy Spirit. Here, in this verse Jesus is telling the apostles to tarry in Jerusalem until the empowering of the Holy Spirit (promise of the father) had been given."

"Why is that so important, Grandpa?" asked Sarah.

"Because, Sarah, it is not enough to be prepared to serve the Lord by just knowing what the will for God is. It is not enough to be prepared by knowing what a Christian should do mentally. In order to be able to do a spiritual work WE MUST BE EQUIPPED SPIRITUALLY. Overlooking this most important point is why most Christians fail in their Christian service."

"Jesus is telling the disciples; that I have equipped you by personally training you in the scriptures and in the mechanical working of the ministry. **But that is not enough. You need the empowering of the Holy Spirit**; so tarry in Jerusalem until you are endued with power from on high."

"Praying every day …THINE IS THE POWER is God's way of reminding the workers of their need of divine power."(+)

MAN FORGETS HIS GREAT NEED OF POWER

"Man has a natural tendency to forget that he personally needs the empowering of the Holy Spirit in order to succeed as a Christian. He learns the doctrines of the Bible, the mechanics of the church and Christian life, and **soon becomes self sufficient**."(+)

MAN FORGETS THE ADMONITION OF JESUS

"One of the last things Jesus preached in his final message as he was going to the garden, and then on to the cross, was on fruit bearing in John chapter 15."(+)

"In that message he warns of God's primary will of getting people Saved. He gave both the positive and the negative in that message."

"Jesus is telling the disciples; that I have equipped you by personally training you in the scriptures and in the mechanical working of the ministry. **But that is not enough. You need the empowering of the Holy Spirit**; so tarry in Jerusalem until you are endued with power from on high."

"The positive was to glorify God by abiding in Christ and bearing much fruit, (+) and one did that by getting many people saved."

"The negative was in speaking of God's discipline on the non-fruitful members and his purging of them in order to help them win more souls or bear more fruit."

"The constant theme of this message was, "WITHOUT ME YE CAN DO NOTHING" that is the punch line of abide in me and let my word abide in you, because without me, ye can do nothing."

"He illustrates this great truth vividly a few days later in the life of these apostles. They had fished all night and CAUGHT NOTHING! But when Jesus told them to let down the nets they caught 153 giant fish."

"There were so many fish they had to drag them out on the shore. (John 21:14) Without Him they caught no fish but with him they caught so many fish they had to drag them to shore."

"Jesus said, "I will build my church." He uses people to do the work, but he is the one who energizes the disciples through the power of the Holy Spirit."

MAN FORGETS THE POWER OF HIS ENEMY

Another reason the child of God needs divine power is because of the strength of the devil. In Ephesians 6:10 Paul admonishes his

HE ANSWERS PRAYER
I Believe God Answers prayer,
Answers always, everywhere;
I may cast my anxious care,
Burdens I could never bear,
On the God who heareth prayer.
Never need my soul despair
Since He bids me boldly dare
To the secret place repair,
There to prove He answers prayer.

brethren "to be strong in the Lord and the power (explosive energy) of his might."

"In verse 11 he tells why, "That ye may be able to stand against the **wiles** (methods of attack) of the devil."(+) The great warrior of the Lord warned, "For we wrestle not against flesh and blood, but against principalities (strong forces) against powers (evil) against the rulers (powerful ones) of the darkness of the world, against spiritual wickedness (satanic filled men) in high places."

"Because of this powerful foe we must put on the whole armor of God, which he describes in the following verses, in order to quench all the fiery darts of the wicked, (literally, the wicked one or the devil.)"

"Verse 18 is the strongest verse commanding prayer in the Bible. Praying always with all prayer and supplication in the Spirit, and watching thereunto with all perseverance and supplication for all saints;"

"Why? Because of the strong forces of the devil which only the Holy Spirit's power can overcome. When Jesus put the phase...THINE IS THE POWER into the model prayer, it was to serve as a constant reminder of our foes and how we can overcome them.(Only through the power of the Holy Spirit)"(+)

EXAMPLES OF THE APOSTLES

"During the time surrounding the period that Jesus was in the grave, and before his resurrection, one can find the apostles in the upper room **behind locked doors**. They were scared to death!"

"A few days before his crucifixion Jesus had to break up an argument between the apostles on who would be the greatest in the kingdom."(+)

"Really, Grandpa where is that found in the bible?" Asked Sarah in wonderment. "That account of their friction concerning who would be the greatest is found in three places, but the actual verse that states this is **Mark 9:33-34** "And he came to Capernaum: and being in the house he asked them, what was it that ye disputed among yourselves by the way?" But they held their peace: for by the way they had disputed among themselves, who [should be] the greatest."

"Before Jesus ascended back to heaven, and before the apostles went to the upper room to "tarry" and "pray", **seven of the apostles had decided to go back to their commercial fishing business**."

"After the "tarrying", and being endued with power of the Holy Spirit, these same men **were fearless**."(+)

"When threatened with death or beatings, they went to the Lord for a fresh enduement of power, and returned to the streets and attacked their persecutor with the gospel."

"When the apostles prayed the model prayer every day in later years and came to the part... **Thine is the power**; it rekindled the knowledge of God's great enabling power which caused them to preach with continual boldness and power."

LUKE'S DIVINE COMMENTARY

"Kids, remember when Grandpa pointed out Matthew's divine commentary concerning unforgiveness?"

"After the "tarrying", and being endued with power of the Holy Spirit, these same men **were fearless**."

"Yes, you said that unforgiveness would lead to bitterness which was worse than cancer," answered Sarah.

"Good, complimented Grandpa. Luke also was moved by the Holy Spirit to give two admonitions that are so vital in Christian lives."

"Immediately after the model prayer Luke gives a story that teaches two great lessons about prayer. This story covers nine verses which are found in Luke 11:5-13."

"Tim, read those verse for us."

*"And he said unto them, Which of you shall have a friend, and shall go unto him at midnight, and say unto him, Friend, lend me three loaves; For a friend of mine in his journey is come to me, and I have nothing to set before him? And he from within shall answer and say, Trouble me not: the door is now shut, and my children are with me in bed; I cannot rise and give thee. I say unto you, Though he will not rise and give him, because he is his friend, yet because of his importunity he will rise and give him as many as he needeth. And I say unto you, **Ask, and it shall be given you; seek, and ye shall find; knock, and it shall be opened unto you.** For every*

one that asketh receiveth; and he that seeketh findeth; and to him that knocketh it shall be opened. If a son shall ask bread of any of you that is a father, will he give him a stone? Or if [he ask] a fish, will he for a fish give him a serpent? Or if he shall ask an egg, will he offer him a scorpion? If ye then, being evil, know how to give good gifts unto your children: HOW MUCH MORE SHALL [YOUR] HEAVENLY FATHER GIVE THE HOLY SPIRIT TO THEM THAT ASK HIM?"

"The two lessons in which he stresses prayer are; to be **persistent in one's prayer life** until God answers the prayer and the persistence of prayer, is found in the simple command of Jesus, "ask and ye shall receive; seek (put legs on your prayers) and ye shall find and **knock (keep on knocking) and it shall be open unto you."** Jesus, speaking of receiving the good gift (God's enabling power), tells the apostles to keep asking for, seeking after, and knocking on **God's door until the good gift is given."**

WHAT DOES IT MEAN, ASK FOR THE HOLY SPIRIT?

"Grandpa, I still don't comprehend why a person has to do all that to receive the Holy Spirit." "All of what, Sarah?" Ask Grandpa. "Well, to ask and seek....and knock," responded Sarah.

"There are two things which you need to understand," replied Grandpa. "When a person is born again, **the Holy Spirit comes unto the person and lives in that person, and he has all of the Holy Spirit that he will ever have."**

"Then why did Jesus say that God would give the Holy Spirit to those who ask for it?" Questioned Tim. "I guess I am confused also"

"The Subject under consideration in this verse has to do with the "GIFT" OF THE HOLY SPIRIT, that is the HOLY SPIRIT'S EMPOWERING OF THE SAVED PERSON FOR SOUL WINNING AND CHRISTIAN SERVICE."

"The direct answer to your question Sarah, as to why the Lord requires people to ask, seek, and knock in order for them to get their prayers answered, is to illustrate **that its God's work,** and it is the Spirit's job to do **the Lord's work through his people**. Remember, we have already quoted Jesus as saying, "For with out me you (the Saved) can to nothing."

Remember, we have already shown in our past lesson that a saved person's **greatest tendency is to trust in his own ability,** instead of looking to and asking God to help and direct him."

> ### Indispensable Christians
>
> "He is impossible to get along with, because he thinks he's impossible to get along without," was said of a Sunday School worker. No wonder the results was a dismal failure for the would-be indispensable. The worst idea a Christian can have is that he is absolutely necessary to the work in which he is engaged, that his absence would stop the whole undertaking.
>
> -Sunday at Home

"Notice once again. "ASK", that means the person is to look to God for an answer." (+)

"SEEK", that is the saved person's job in complying with what the bible teaches for him to do in order for God to see the sincerity of his prayers, while he is asking and looking to God for answers."

"KNOCK indicates that a child of God is to trust in the Lord, do his will, and believe that God will answer his prayer according to his wisdom and timing. In so doing the child of God acknowledges his inability and **demonstrates his faith in God** to answer his prayers."

"**The apostles were all saved** when Jesus commanded them to "**tarry in the city of Jerusalem**" until they were endued with power form on high."

"Let me try and illustrate why one must ask God for the Holy Spirit in order to succeed as a soul winner and Christian. Tim, do you see that pot that your grandma filled with soil?"

The **asking** is the **prayer,** the **seeking** is doing all in one's own power to aid in the answer of the prayer, and the **knocking** teaches persistence.

"Yes," replied Tim.

"What would you have to do before you could fill that pot with water?"

"He would **have to empty the pot** of the soil before he could fill it with water, right grandpa?" Came Sarah's answer.

"That's right, Sarah. Most people are like that pot. **They are already full**, but they are not full of the Holy Spirit. **They are full of their own interest** or they are **full of the world**. They may even want their prayers answered in order to take the credit or to satisfy their own desires. So the asking, seeking in prayer is to help them realize that they have to **fully depend on God** in order to be filled or empowered by the Holy Spirit."

"They have to empty themselves in order to be filled with the Holy Spirit, is that right Grandpa?", asked Sarah.

"Yes, that's true Sarah. God wants to hear and answer their prayers. God wants to use them to get others saved, but God knows every persons heart, and he gives them spiritual exercises to perform in order for them to grow in faith as a Christian."

"THEY HAVE ALL OF THE HOLY SPIRIT BUT THE HOLY SPIRIT DOES NOT HAVE ALL OF THEM." "They must empty themselves in order to be filled or empowered of the Holy Spirit. Praying every day, **"Thine is the power,"** is God's way of reminding his children that they must have Gods power in order to have their prayers answered, **especially to be filled with the Holy Spirit."**

"The **asking** is the **prayer,** the **seeking** is doing all in one's own power to aid in the answer of the prayer, and the **knocking** teaches persistence. Keep asking, and seeking, asking, seeking, until the prayer is answered. Is that right Grandpa?," asked Tim.(+)

"That's right, Tim it is so sad that many people give up on their prayers before God's promised answer comes."

"Is that what Jesus meant when He said, you'll reap, if you faint not?" asked Sarah.

"That's close Sarah, Paul said, "let us not be weary in well doing: for in due season we shall reap, if faint not." (Galatians 6:9) But Jesus did say, "that men should always pray, and not faint" (Luke 18:1)

"You understand the point Sarah, you just quoted the wrong person," added Tim. "But what is the inspired point that Luke is making in those verses?"

"The second inspired comment on the model prayer refers directly to this lesson. "THINE IS... THE POWER." This principle is found in Luke 11:13. This verse speaks of God giving this

When one prays "**Thine is the Kingdom**" it reminds him of the defense, which conquers these thoughts, is the Word of God. The devil attacks through the mind and the Christian takes his shield (the Word of God) and quotes a verse that overcomes that thought.

divine power. Remember, the previous verses are teaching persistence in prayer with the inducement of doing everything in his power to bring about the answer of prayer. Tim read the verse and promise for yourself."

"If ye then, being evil (meaning having a depraved nature) know how to give good gifts unto your children: how much more shall your heavenly father give the Holy Spirit to them that ask him? THINE IS THE POWER means that Jesus has all power, and he has promised to give that enabling power to any person **who really wants it."**

THINE IS...THE POWER TO OVERCOME

"In Ephesians 6:16 Paul commands the believer to take the shield of faith (Word of God), in order to quench all the fiery darts that the devil shoots into his mind."

"Kids, the devil attacks the Believer through his mind. The fiery darts that Paul was referring to were thoughts, which the devil shoots into the believer's mind."(+)

He shoots thoughts of unbelief.
He shoots thoughts of rebellion.
He shoots thoughts of fear.
He shoots thoughts of lust.
He shoots thoughts, which attack the truths of the Scriptures." (+)

"The vivid example of this is when the devil attacked Jesus after his baptism when he was very weak because he had fasted (went with out food or water) for 40 days. Each time the devil attacked Jesus; Jesus would take the shield of faith (the Word of God) and defeat the devil by quoting and obeying the scriptures."

"When one prays "**Thine is the Kingdom**" it reminds him of the defense, which conquers these thoughts, is the Word of God. The devil attacks through the mind and the Christian takes his shield (the Word of God) and quotes a verse that overcomes that thought."

"Kids, there is a statement which I want you to remember."

"What is it Grandpa?," came their reply.

"One should always believe the **great promises in the Word of God** and not his doubts or dumb thoughts."(+) Grandpa admonished.

VIVID ILLUSTRATION

"Look what believing ones fears and dumb thoughts instead of God's sure and immutable promises will cause."

"The devil spooked ten of the twelve spies, which Moses sent to spy out the Promise Land. This caused Israel to draw back to great destruction. It changed the course of Jewish history as they wandered aimlessly in the wilderness of Sin instead of crossing over the Jordan River victoriously."

A GREAT VICTORY

"Do you have a positive example of someone who believed God's word?" Inquired Sarah.

"Yes, the Devil attacked Gideon through his mind and made him feel weak and unable to deliver his nation from bondage. God, giving Gideon assurances through the Word of God, and Gideon quenched all the fiery darts of the Devil and won one of Israel's greatest victories."

"We can overcome the devil in the same way, cant we Grandpa?" asked Sarah.

"By believing God and trusting him for his power, right Grandpa?" answered Tim

"Right", affirmed Grandpa. "Kids, there is one more principle which I want to cover before our lesson is over today."

"What is that, Grandpa?" asked Sarah

"It is about man's inferiority complex, and how to overcome it."

"Good", responded both of the students.

OVERCOMING AN INFERIORITY COMPLEX

"Every man has an inferiority complex to some degree", continued Grandpa, "and the devil attacks us through our minds in order to neutralize us or cause us to draw back in unbelief."

"Jesus is well aware of our weaknesses! **We don't attempt great things, because we are aware of our weaknesses and our shortcomings.** BUT HE HAS ALL POWER!"(+)

"He promises to give his children the Holy Spirit power if they will only ask him and meet his conditions of empowering."

"The little expression in the model prayer of "THINE IS...THE POWER" was placed there to reassure the believer every day that God, who cannot lie, has promised to give that enabling power to any of his children who will earnestly ask him."

"Through his power WE CAN BE STRONG in the Lord and THE POWER OF HIS MIGHT!"(+)

"Wow, Grandpa!   That's great!" exclaimed Sarah.

"Any homework?" asked Tim.

"Yes, I want you to read the fourth and the fifth chapters of Revelation, TWICE."

"TWICE?" the kids echoed.

"Yes, not once but twice," laughed Grandpa!

> **We don't attempt great things, because we are aware of our weaknesses and our shortcomings**. BUT HE HAS ALL POWER!

POINTS TO PONDER

❖ **Thine is the Power means; the Holy Spirit's power is for CHRISTIAN SERVICE.**

❖ **God CANNOT fill me if I am full of the world.**

❖ **God CANNOT fill me if I am full of Self.**

❖ **God WILL NOT fill me unless I earnestly desire his power for his Glory.**

❖ **Although I am weak and unable, he has promised me his enabling power.**

❖ **I can do all things THROUGH CHRIST which strengtheneth me.**

Lesson Eleven

AFTER THIS MANNER THEREFORE PRAY YE: *Our Father which art in heaven, Hallowed be thy name. Thy kingdom come. Thy will be done in earth, as [it is] in heaven. Give us this day our daily bread. And forgive us our debts, as we forgive our debtors. And lead us not into temptation, but deliver us from evil: For thine is the kingdom, and the power, and THE GLORY, forever.*
AMEN.
Matthew 6:9-13

Lesson Eleven
THINE IS...THE GLORY

"Hello children. It is good to see your smiling faces."

"We did our homework, Grandpa. In fact I believe Tim read the chapters three times," reported Sarah.

"Good boy. You kids have been a blessing to me, but our subject is so massive today that we better get right to it."

CREATED TO GLORIFY GOD

"Kids, did you know that you were created for GOD'S PLEASURE AND DELIGHT?" (+)

"Yes," answered Sarah. "That information was given in the homework you gave us."

"I didn't know that," responded Tim, "until I read it in the Bible. The twenty-four elders cast their crowns down before Jesus' throne and shouted...."

"Let me read it, Tim," interrupted his sister.

"Thou art worthy, O Lord, to receive glory and honor and power. For thou hath created all things, and for **THY PLEASURE THEY ARE AND WERE CREATED.**" (+)

"That verse states that the reason God created all things, including man, was and is for his pleasure or delight."

"I never thought about that before. THAT I WAS CREATED FOR GOD'S PLEASURE," Tim confessed.

"No, I never thought about that either. I always wanted my way and most of the time, I must confess, God wasn't even in my thoughts," Sarah said rather sadly. (+)

"All of us have the same tendency kids, until we get into God's word and begin to obey its teaching. In Proverbs 12:22 the wise man states, they that deal truly (according to God's Word) are his (God's) delight."

GLORIFY GOD IN ALL THINGS

"Grandpa, I want to glorify or please the Lord in my life, especially since we have been having our studies, but how can I do it? I'm just a young girl and I don't know much about the Bible."

"I'm not a young girl, but I feel the same way Sarah does. Grandpa, can you give us some rules to follow?" asked Tim.

"Kids, this question has been asked by many, many people. There are two verses that I will give you. The first one is I Corinthians 10:31. Tim, turn there and read it for us."

Tim reads, "Whether therefore ye eat, or drink, or whatsoever ye do, DO ALL TO THE GLORY OF GOD." (+)

"Kids, we should live our lives trying to please God. He gave us life and he continues to give us life day by day. Always remember why he gave us our lives."

"For his pleasure," responded both young people.

"We should think, before getting involved with events or things- **will this give God pleasure?** It states 'whatsoever you do—Do all to the glory of God."

"But Grandpa, that doesn't sound like much fun," objected Sarah.

"Sarah, when you realize it is your heavenly Father's will to give you good gifts and in John 10:10 Jesus boldly revealed why he (Jesus) came into the world. He said, 'I am come that they might have life (eternal life or be saved) and that **they might have it more abundantly.'"**

"Jesus wants to give you the abundant life. That means he wants to give you a victorious life, and make you a champion and an over-comer of all situations. Believe me girl; if you give your life to Jesus, **you will live an exciting and happy life**."

Tim speaks to his sister, "Grandpa ought to know, Sarah. He and Grandma have been living for the Lord over forty years and are two of the happiest old people...sorry Grandpa... that I know."

"They sure are," confessed Sarah.

"The other scripture is also in I Corinthians. In I Corinthians 6:19-20 the Bible says that our body is the temple (living place) of the Holy Spirit. Then note the last five words in verse nineteen, 'Ye are not your own' in other words, you don't belong to yourself anymore. Verse twenty explains why."

> "Whether therefore ye eat, or drink, or whatsoever ye do, DO ALL TO THE GLORY OF GOD."

"For you are bought with a price: (the precious blood of Jesus). Therefore, Glorify God in your BODY, and in your SPIRIT WHICH ARE GOD'S."   (+)

"These two verses teach us that when we accepted Jesus as our Savior we were born of the Holy Spirit who now resides within each believer. We voluntarily ask God to save us on the grounds that we would live for Him. He bought us with the death of Jesus, and now we are to glorify him in our body and spirit which are his."

"Our first principle in our study of THINE IS THE GLORY is that we were created TO GIVE GOD PLEASURE."

WAYS TO GLORIFY GOD

"You are right, kids" confessed Grandpa, "But more than that, during all those years that your grandmother and I have served the Lord, I have never met one single person who regretted being a Christian. Many of them regretted not being a more devoted

186

Christian but not one ever expressed a regret for becoming a Christian."

"Now, let me ask you, how are some of the ways that we can glorify God in our body and spirit?" Grandpa continued.

THE THING WHICH REALLY GIVES GOD GLORY

"First, kids, let me ask you what you think is the primary way of glorifying God?"

"That's easy," said Sarah. "It is in our praise service."

"God may get glory out of some praise services but I have my doubts about two or three churches I've been to with my friends," stated Tim.

"Why is that Tim?" asked Grandpa.

"Well, I don't mean to sound judgmental Grandpa, but if God doesn't get more out of it than I do…they sing the same things over and over again and if it wasn't for the words in the song you would think you were somewhere in the world."

> **"Ye are not your own'** other wise, you don't belong to yourself anymore. Verse twenty explains why, for you are bought with a price: (the precious blood of Jesus). Therefore, Glorify God in your BODY, and in your SPIRIT WHICH ARE GOD'S."

"Tim, I didn't know that you felt that way," remarked Sarah.

"Well this is the first time any one ever asked me. While I am…"

"Preaching," interjected Sarah.

"I am not preaching," defended Tim. "But, I thought that the music service in the church was to glorify God. Much of what I have seen seems to be directed more toward the flesh. Grandpa, you said we are to glorify God in everything we do—that should be especially true when it comes to singing and worshipping God." (+)

"Grandpa, I just heard you say," responded Sarah. Then she caught her mistake. "No, the Bible said whatsoever you do—do all to the glory of God."

"**Right**," agreed Grandpa. "Before we get to the first principle which really glorifies God may I explain the part that music plays in church services? Music is to prepare the hearts of people for the Word of God which the pastor will preach following the song service. (+) Now let's get to the Bible and see what really gives God glory?"

> ### What do these have in common?
>
> "Looking unto Jesus, the author and finisher of our faith"
> "WHEN YE PRAY SAY"
> "obey them that have the rule over you...for they watch for your souls"
>
> ### They are all commandments of God!

"Sarah read John 15:8 for us," continued Grandpa.

"John, chapter fifteen, verse eight," stated Sarah, as she began to read. "Herein is my father glorified that we bear much fruit; so shall we be his disciples". What does that mean, BEAR MUCH FRUIT, Grandpa?"

"God created everything to bring fruit after its own kind. Apple trees bear apples after its kind. When two young people get married, it is natural for them to have children. Solomon stated that, The fruit of the righteous (children of God) is a tree of life; then he reaffirms that principle by saying **he that winneth souls is wise** (Proverbs 11:30)."

"A tree that does not produce fruit for itself, but for others. The tree that Solomon is talking about is a tree producing life to others. He is affirming that a righteous person's (one who is saved) **fruit is getting others saved**."

"The primary reason Jesus came into the world was to glorify his Father. The primary way he glorified his father was by getting people saved. In this chapter on fruit bearing Jesus tells the apostles that the way they are to glorify God is by **getting many people saved**." (+)

"So, Sarah, the way God gets the greatest Glory is not through talk or even singing. It is helping people to understand they are sinners, that they are lost, that God so loved them that he gave his Son Jesus to die in their place, so they could turn from their sins and trust him as their Savior."

"Jesus gave his life to save sinners and when WE GET SINNERS SAVED IT GLORIFIES GOD."

"Every child of God was designed by God to be a Tree of Life that is bearing fruit (sinners). Solomon reaffirms that truth by commenting, and he that winneth souls is wise."

"Grandpa, does that mean that if Tim and I are not winning souls that we are not glorifying God?" asked Sarah.

"No, replied Grandpa. We will show you other ways for a child of God to glorify God in their lives. **But—now get this— winning souls is what God expects you to do.** Winning souls is a child of God's purpose or birthright, just as children are the natural purpose or birthright of marriage. (+) The rest of verse 15, which you read Sarah, states, so shall ye be my disciples."

"When a person sees Christians winning souls there is no doubt that they are of God. Good apples from a tree prove the tree to be a good apple tree. People who bear fruit (get people saved) prove they are saved and are disciples or followers of God."

"You prove you are a Christian by getting other people saved," affirmed Tim.(+)

"Yes," replied Grandpa, "and at the same time, you are giving God pleasure as well as glorifying him."

GLORIFY GOD BY DOING GOOD WORKS

"In Matthew 5:16, Jesus gives another way for a child of God to glorify his Father. Tim, you read the verse this time. It is Matthew 5:16."

"Let your light so shine before men, that they may see your good works, and glorify your Father in heaven." (+)

"May I quickly list some good works that a Christian may do which will glorify God?"

"It is more a way of life than doing one good work now and some other good thing at a later time. It is a consistent daily walk before the world (neighbors and friends)." (+)

"A child of God ought to be baptized and **become faithful to all the church services.** He is to implement what he learns about the Christian life and practice them in his daily walk with Christ."

"He is to ask what Jesus would do in each situation and then do his best to obey Jesus."

"His attitude should be kind and full of mercy and truth. He abstains from things of the world, such as questionable practices and language."

"If a person lives that way it will not be long before people see his good deeds, kind spirit and Christ-like walk. They will realize that person is different. It will cause some to glorify God when they witness your daily, Christ-like walk. But, this Christ-like walk will bring some criticism and even persecution."(+)

"Peter speaks of how a Christian should react when he is reproached for his service for Christ. If ye be reproached for the name of Christ, happy are ye; for the spirit of glory and of God resteth upon you: on their part he is evil spoken of, but on your part he is glorified."

"Yet if any man suffer as a Christian let him not be ashamed, but let him glorify God on this behalf."

> **Winning souls is what God expects you to do.** Winning souls is a child of God's purpose or birthright, just as children are the natural purpose or birthright of marriage.

"Kids, when a person really takes a stand and lives for God he will run into some problems."

Sarah looks at Tim and says, "We have already experienced some of that. But what are some of the other ways we can glorify the Lord?"

GLORIFY GOD BY THE WAY YOU DIE

"Solomon stated a principle in Ecclesiastes that there was a proper time for everything. He became specific when he stated, a time to be born and a time to die. Ecclesiastes 3:2"

"Barring the second coming of Christ everyone on planet earth will die. All past human beings were born, lived a short time, and then died."

"We all know we are going to die. We should choose to glorify God in our life and glorify God in our death. Jesus, in John 21:18-19 speaks of the way apostle Peter would glorify God in his death. The words he spoke in verse 18 signifying BY WHAT DEATH HE (PETER) SHOULD GLORIFY GOD (speaking of his death)."

"This is a very important point. Don't just think that death is for old people, and pass over this marvelous truth."

"Each one of us should determine that we are going to glorify God through our death, if God should determine that we should die."

"If you should die with cancer or with a twisted, mangled body through disease or accident and suffer indescribable pain, determine you will die in a way that will glorify God. **Let your focus be on Him**. Radiate his love and grace to the doctors, nurses, family members, and friends. God can use not only your lips to praise him but God's grace in your life while you suffer and die, can also be a great source of praise to the Lord."

OLD PEOPLE CAN GLORIFY GOD

"A dear preacher friend at 88 years of age commented, "these birthdays are going to kill me if I don't stop having them." Sure enough they did. But he was one of the most faithful men, in the church and lived the most daily Christ-centered life, I have ever known. He had suffered a car accident when he was in his mid-70s that took his wife's life, and caused him to suffer physical pain until he died in church on Wednesday a night in his 89th year. Because of that faithful life **people were saved at his funeral**. He left a faithful life for his family and many others to follow." (+)

"Proverbs 16:31 testifies of the life of M. B. Hubbard, the man in the above paragraph, and older people who persevere by going to church through bad weather, and in spite of their personal pain and discomfort. The verse states, The hoary head is a **crown of glory, IF IT BE FOUND IN THE WAY OF RIGHTEOUSNESS.**"

"A faithful life of love to the Savior, manifested in the lives of older people that may have difficulty walking physically, but manifest a spring in the step as they follow in the light of God's spiritual walk, brings tremendous glory to their God." (+)

"A good summary of one glorifying God is found in Psalms 150:6. There the Bible states Let everything that hath breath praise the Lord. **Praise ye the Lord.**"

THINE IS THE GLORY, A HEART MATTER

"Please note that the expression THINE IS THE GLORY is next to last in God's order in the model prayer."

"It is to be done by individuals on a day-by-day basis. Jesus explained that God was seeking people who would worship Him in **Spirit and in truth**. John 4."

"In Isaiah 1:11-15, the prophet quotes God as saying that their religious service was an abomination to God and he would not accept it as praise and worship. The primary thing for one to always remember is that praise to God—(that which glorifies God) is a **heart matter** and not something which appeals to the flesh."

"That helps me, Grandpa. PRAISE IS A HEART MATTER AND NOT SOMETHING THAT APPEALS TO THE FLESH," echoed Tim.

TESTIMONIES TO THINE IS...THE GLORY

"Kids, I want to show you that God has always been glorified. Throughout time and back into the

194

infinite past, there have been those that have praised his holy name." (+)

"In Colossians, Paul writes" "For by him were all things created, that are in heaven, and that are in earth, visible and invisible, whether they be thrones, or dominions, or principalities, or powers: all things were created by him, and for him: and he is before all things, and by him all things consist."

"Then Paul concludes that because he made all things, holds all things together, and has redeemed all things to God; through his death and resurrection, HE IS TO HAVE THE PREEMINENCE IN ALL THINGS."

THE ANGELS GLORIFIED HIM

"God was teaching Job about the awesome feats of God in the creation of this universe, and gave the reactions of the angels as they witnessed this marvelous performance."

"When the MORNING STARS SANG TOGETHER and all the sons of God (angels) SHOUTED FOR JOY!"

"It sounds like the angels were a gigantic cheering section! God lays the foundation of the earth and the angels

How to Save

The story is told of a man who contributed the money to build a church. Later on he lost all his property. "If you had the money you put into that church." Someone said to him, "you could start again." But the good man wisely replied: "That is the only money I have saved. If I had not given it to the Lord it would have gone with the rest. Now it will always be mine." — Moody Monthly

applaud his magnificent work. He cast the stars into orbit and they catch their breath in wonderment. When He orders the sun into place and begins his **daily travels,** the angels' break into songs of praise. He places the waters of the seas into their places and commands their limits. The heavenly host could not stand it any longer as they shout and sang as they witness their Lord and Master in his glorious work." (+)

"The inspired psalmist gives an account of that glorious day. *"Praise ye the LORD. Praise ye the LORD from the heavens: praise him in the heights. Praise ye him, all his angels: praise ye him, all his hosts. Praise ye him, sun and moon: praise him, all ye stars of light. Praise him, ye heavens of heavens, and ye waters that be above the heavens. Let them praise the name of the LORD: for he commanded, and they were created."* Psalm 148:1-5" (+)

GOD IS GRACIOUS TO ALL LIVING CREATURES

"The whole earth is filled with birds and animals who are fed and cared for daily by their gracious God. "Tim, read Psalm 145:15-16, *'The eyes of all wait upon thee; and thou givest them their meat in due season. Thou openest thine hand, and satisfiest the desire of every living thing."*

"I've never thought about that before," exclaimed Tim! "How awesome"

"Sarah read Psalm 148:7 for us."

Sarah begins by stating "Psalms, chapter 148, verse 7."

"Praise the Lord from the earth, ye dragons, and all deeps."

"In verse 10 the Psalmist continues, *"Beast and all cattle: creeping things and flying fowl."* In verse thirteen he concludes by saying, **"Let them praise the name of the Lord."**

> For his name alone is excellent, HIS GLORY is above all the earth and heaven

"Kids, sometimes I love to just sit or lie in bed and hear MY FAITHFUL FRIENDS praise the Lord." (+)

"Your faithful friends, Grandpa? Who are they?" inquired Sarah.

"Sarah, they are the little feathered creatures that God placed on this earth to teach us to praise him."

"The birds?" Tim responded in surprise.

"Yes, Tim, develop the habit of taking time to enjoy their music."

"I hear one singing outside my window and interpret his sweet notes, and in my mind I hear him sing, **'All hail the power of Jesus name, let angels prostrate fall. Bring forth the royal diadems and crown him Lord of all."**

"At another time I hear one sing, 'Whatsoever things are true, **think on these things**. Whatsoever things are honest, **think on these things**. Whatsoever things are just, **think on these things**. Whatsoever things are pure, **think on these things**. Whatsoever things are lovely, **think on these things**. Whatsoever things are of good report **think on these things** and if there be any virtue, and if there be any praise **think on these things**. Those things, which ye have both learned, and received, and heard, and seen in me, do: And the God of peace will be with you. (Philippians 4:8-9) And the God of peace will not only keep you but the God of peace will also bless you. Hallelujah and glory to his name."

"Oh, Grandpa, do you do that, really?" inquired Sarah.

"Sarah, often times I do," confessed Grandpa.

"I've often wondered why the birds were so happy!" exclaimed Tim.

"THEY ARE HAPPY BECAUSE THEY SPEND ALL THEIR TIME PRAISING THE LORD." (+)

"Yes, confirmed Grandpa, that is the reason I call them MY FAITHFUL FRIENDS. They have helped me to be more faithful in praising the Lord."

"For his name alone is excellent, HIS GLORY is above all the earth and heaven."

"**KIDS, THE TIME WILL COME WHEN EVEN GOD'S ENEMIES WILL PRAISE HIS HOLY NAME.**" (Rom.14: 11, Is. 45:23-25)

CHRIST'S GREATEST GLORY IN TIME

"Now students, lets go over the chapters which I assigned as your home work."

Tim, said, "I was wondering when we would get to that."

"Me too," commented Sarah.

"I had you read the fourth and fifth chapters of Revelation."

"Twice," both of the kids commented.

"The fourth chapter begins with the rapture of the saints, and many things take place; joy, commendations, and glory. Those who are rewarded, turn right around and acknowledge where the true glory should be given by casting their crowns at the feet of Jesus."

"Chapter five begins by revealing an APPARENT PROBLEM IN HEAVEN. While there was joy and victory at the awards banquet, there was total devastation, death and destruction taking place on earth. The angels could not find anyone who could legally stop the destruction on earth."

"John began to weep." The scripture states, "he wept much."

"Then Jesus, as The Lion of the Tribe of Judah, the root (human descendant of King David) and the eternal Son of God, stepped forward."

"The elders, the living creature, the angels and all the host of heaven, recognized Jesus as the earth's

Kinsman Redeemer, with the power to dethrone the Devil as the God of this age, and throw him into hell."

"The purpose stated in Genesis of man ruling over the earth **was about to become reality.**" (Gen. 1:26)

"The Prophet Daniel's prophecy of the Corner Stone crushing all Kingdoms and establishing an everlasting kingdom **was about to come to pass.**" (Dan. 2:44) (+)

"Isaiah's announcement of the purpose of the birth of Jesus to establish a righteous government of the world **is about to begin.**"

"The endless reign of peace and righteousness was commencing." (Isaiah. 9:6-7)

"With these wonderful, victorious events unfolding, **it was just too much** for the thousands of ten thousands of millions there in heaven to contain."

"First, a few begin to sing a new song. IT WAS PRAISE TO THE LAMB."

"**It was a song of redemption** which every kindred and tongue and people and nation could sing. **It was praise** for elevating them to positions where they could serve him as priests and kings." (Rev. 5:9)

"Then the angels who were created to praise the Lord **burst into praise** (v.10). There was such a host that they could not be numbered."

"All the accumulated battles, through all the long and bitter centuries were coming to an end. Their champion had overcome all enemies and in righteousness is now ready to take the role of KING OF KINGS AND LORD OF LORDS."

"Because of this overwhelming victory the angels begin to sing in a loud voice."

"Their Song; Worthy is the Lamb that was slain to receive power (authority) and riches and wisdom and Glory and Blessing" (+)

"Grandpa, I can almost hear the Hallelujah chorus, whispered Sarah.

> All the accumulated battles, through all the long and bitter centuries were coming to an end. Their champion had overcome all enemies and in righteousness is now ready to take the role of KING OF KINGS AND LORD OF LORDS

"It is such a praise song!   Verse thirteen describes the singing. As everyone on the earth sings, then those under the earth join the praises as voices join voices and still others. Those that are in the sea begin to sing until the whole heavens vibrate with the Holy Choruses. The words are simple."

They were saying:

"BLESSED AND HONOR AND GLORY AND POWER"

To Whom?

"TO THE ONE SITTING ON THE THRONE AND TO THE LAMB FOREVER AND EVER".

"There is that hallelujah chorus again, Grandpa," repeated Sarah.

"The four living creatures said **amen, amen, amen, amen**! The 24 elders fell down and worshiped him. This is no doubt the greatest moment of praise that God ever received in the history of man - Only He knows what a great times await in the millennium and on into the eternal ages to come." (+)

ARROWS POINTING TOWARD HEAVEN

"Kids, think about what the last few words in THE MODEL PRAYER ARE POINTING TOWARD... NOTE THEM:

Thine is the Kingdom
Thine is the Power
Thine is the Glory
Forever!!"

"Those words are all pointing toward..."Grandpa pauses.

"Toward the future!" exclaimed Sarah.

> This is no doubt the greatest moment of praise that God ever received in the history of man

"Toward the millennium," spoke Tim.

"They are pointing toward heaven!" cried Sarah.

"The eternal ages," stated Tim.

"When one prays the model prayer with understanding of its purposes and message, it is designed to lift ones mind off the troubles and trials of earth, and fasten them on the coming kingdom and GLORY."

"When one prays, THINE IS THE GLORY it is like FLAMING ARROWS POINTING TOWARD HEAVEN, isn't it Grandpa?" exclaimed Sarah. (+)

"What a way of expressing it, Sarah," complimented Tim.

"But there is one thing that mystifies me," humbly stated Grandpa.

THINE IS ... THE GLORY
THE MYSTERY OF THINE IS ... THE GLORY

"I will close our study on THINE IS ... THE GLORY by revealing something that mystifies me."

"I can't understand why God loves poor lost sinners like me so, much that he gave his son to die in my place. How marvelous! That is beyond my ability to understand and explain. Oh, but I am so glad he did! His love is beyond our ability to comprehend. I just accept my good fortune and riches and **work at giving him pleasure and glory.**" (+)

"All the accumulated battles through all the long and bitter centuries were coming to an end. Their champion had overcome all enemies and in righteousness is now ready to take the role of KING OF KINGS AND LORD OF LORDS."

"Kids, your homework for next week is do something special in order to demonstrate THINE IS THE GLORY, which will praise and glorify the Lord."

POINTS TO PONDER

❖ I can glorify God BY WINNING SOULS.

❖ I can glorify God by living a faithful and loving life BEFORE MEN.

❖ I can glorify God in my body by dressing like a Christian.

❖ I was born to give God PLEASURE AND GLORY IN ALL THINGS.

❖ I can even glorify God IN MY DEATH.

Lesson Twelve

AFTER THIS MANNER THEREFORE PRAY YE: Our Father which art in heaven, Hallowed be thy name. Thy kingdom come. Thy will be done in earth, as [it is] in heaven. Give us this day our daily bread. And forgive us our debts, as we forgive our debtors. And lead us not into temptation, but deliver us from evil: For thine is the kingdom, and the power, and the glory, FOREVER. Amen.
-Matthew 6:9-13

ADDITIONAL SCRIPTURE REFERENCE:
Luke 5:5-13

LESSON TWELVE
FOREVER

"Hello Grandpa, Boy, do we have exciting news for you! Our homework assignment was to do something that would really glorify God, "greeted Tim.

"And God really helped us in our efforts to bring him pleasure, joined in Sarah."(+)

"What is it kids? I'm dying to find out?" Asked Grandpa.

"You will have to wait a little while, Grandpa, said Tim. I have a friend who will be here in a few minutes after he gets off work."

"Okay, agreed Grandpa. Let's get right into our lesson. Our lesson today may be the hardest for the human mind to grasp.(+) We have so many things in our lives and in this world that hinder us from really understanding well enough to practice this principle. Only a small percentage, are able to master this principle."

"What is it, Grandpa? Inquired Sarah."

"FOREVER" stated Grandpa.

"FOREVER" echoed both Tim and Sarah.

FOREVER OR ETERNITY

"Yes, forever or eternity."

"That doesn't seem so hard," objected Sarah. "Everyone knows we are going to die and then go into eternity."

"Wait a minute, Sarah. Grandpa said that only a few **master that principle**. He isn't talking about a simple belief in a heaven or a hell."(+)

"That is right, Tim. In order to master the principle of forever or eternity one must first **accept eternity as a fact.** Then that individual must **meditate on that fact until eternity becomes a conviction**. Even after the future existence of life becomes a firm conviction it may not direct one's life.

Our lesson today may be the hardest for the human mind to grasp. We have so many things in our lives and in this world that hinder us from really understanding well enough to practice this principle.

Most people who truly have been saved have a firm conviction there is a heaven and a hell. But **many of those people's lives are not altered much by their beliefs.(+)** But after reading the Bible, prayer, and a life of Christian service, one **begins to be motivated by the reality of eternity, until it controls his life."**

"It took the Old Testament patriarch, Abraham, almost a full lifetime before eternity seized control of his life."

"There were three separate encounters with God over several decades before Abraham's life was fully **directed by eternity**."

"Abraham was not only governed by his belief, but **Abraham's belief was so real that he could see the Holy City** which had twelve foundations, and whose builder and maker was God.(+) His conviction of eternity not only changed his life **but the lives of thousands of others.**

MOSES DEVELOPED THE "FOREVER LOOK"

"Eternity became so real to Moses that he forsook the richest kingdom of the world, and chose to suffer affliction with God's people; esteeming the reproach of Christ is greater riches than the treasures in Egypt."

"Moses saw him who was invisible and had respect unto the recompense of the reward.(+) His mind was fixed on eternity which greatly directed his life. This conviction was developed over a period of several years. In fact, he spent 40 years in Egypt and 40 years on the backside of a desert, before his eyes became fixed on eternity.(+)"

"Grandpa, **thy kingdom come** is much harder for me to comprehend than eternity."

"Sarah, that is probably because the concept is so new to you. But bear in mind the kingdom and its teaching was very familiar to the apostles. **John the Baptist**

> **Time**
> I have only just a minute, only sixty seconds in it, forced upon me –can't refuse it, didn't seek it, didn't choose it, but it's up to me to use it. I must suffer if I lose it; give account if I abuse it. Just a tiny little minute—but, **eternity** is in it!
> -Copied

came preaching the kingdom, and all of the apostles were John's converts. Jesus taught them to seek **first the kingdom of God in their lives."(+)**

"Please note kids, that it wasn't until Jesus taught them about the kingdom for 40 days (Acts 1:3), this principle got down into their hearts and souls and took charge of their lives.(+) They didn't fully realize that their main purpose was to get the Gospel to every creature in the world.(+) Based on doing their best, they would be lifted to a **close fellowship of eating at his table and helping him rule the earth for a thousand years."**

"That is basically the same principle that transformed both Abraham and Moses, wasn't it Grandpa?" Tim asked.

"You are right, Tim, you are so right."

AN EXAMPLE OF THE FRUIT GOD GIVES

"I see a young man coming across the lawn. Is he your friend, Tim?"

"Hi, Eugene, come on in. This is my Grandpa. Eugene is a friend of mine, and has just started coming to our church.

"Welcome, my boy. Have a seat."

Tim stuttered a little as he began to speak. "Our homework last week was to do something that would really glorify God.(+) The verse In John 15 which stated "herein is my Father glorified, that you bring forth much fruit" was in my mind. So I started looking for someone that I could lead to the Lord."

Eugene interrupted, "It was me. For a long time I had really wanted to know about becoming a Christian."

"First, Tim told me I was a sinner. Boy, I knew that already. When he got to the part about the wages of sin was death, or separation from God, I began to get scared."

"Then Tim showed me in the Bible that God loved me, that he had already died on the cross as my substitute. God spoke to my heart and I wanted to be saved."

Both boys were wiping tears from their eyes. "So I asked God to forgive me of my sins **and he did**." The boys embraced each other again.

Grandpa said, "**PRAISE THE LORD!**"

Sarah was beaming with pride because God had used her big brother to lead someone to Christ.

"Grandpa, I want to say that the section under the heading, **Thy will be done in earth as it is in heaven,** helped me the most of any of our lessons. I learned that God's will on this earth as it is in heaven, **is to get people saved from hell.(+)**"

"Oh yes, Grandpa. I'm not taking that good job any more. God wants me to be a preacher, and I'm going to Bible College next fall."

"Wow!" exclaimed Sarah.

"Well, well," commented Grandpa, "what do you know about that!" "I'm going, too!" exclaimed Eugene. "I'm too much of a follower. I need Tim's steady influence and friendship."

After a few more minutes of rejoicing and fellowship, Grandpa said, "we had better get back to our lesson".

CREATED IN THE IMAGE OF GOD

"In Genesis 1:26 God said, let us create man in our image and likeness. God is from everlasting to everlasting or eternal (Psalm 90:2). Since man is created in the image and likeness of eternal God, man is also an eternal being.(+) When Adam sinned the curse of death came upon him and his family, but that did not alter the fact that man was created in the image of God and is eternal."

"The drastic action which God took by offering Jesus on the cross proved that, didn't it Grandpa?" Commented Tim.

"Yes, it should have, but many want to accept that man is eternal only when they believe that man is righteous. If he is not righteous they teach that he is eliminated or ceases to exist when he dies.(+)"

"How can they believe that, Grandpa," asked Sarah?

"**First** they do not understand that man was made in the image of eternal God which makes him an eternal being."

"**Second** they pervert the meaning of the word, **forever**."(+)

INTO THE AGES OF THE AGES

"They refer to the word **forever**, when it is used in reference to earthly life or events, instead of studying the usage of the word when it is dealing with eternal things."

"The New Testament was written in Greek, which was the language the common man spoke in that day. The original Greek word forever is translated "INTO THE AGES OF THE AGES", and refers to the duration of time of those in heaven and the duration of time of those that suffer in hell. The same word is used in reference to both, heaven and hell, **there is no difference.**"

"If Jesus and those in heaven will live **forever** then the language used also teaches that the suffering of those in hell will be forever"(+)

THEY MAKE GOD SOUND CRUEL AND UNCARING

"Grandpa, don't the people who teach that

What do these have in common?

"Lay up for yourselves treasures in heaven"
"WHEN YE PRAY SAY"
"Quench Not The Spirit"

They are all commandments of God!

---

know the truth," asked Tim?

"Tim, the leaders in the groups that deny there is no eternal hell are well educated men. They generally have a good knowledge of the Bible languages...."

"Bible languages?" questioned Sarah.

"Yes, Sarah, when the Bible was written, it was written in Hebrew and Greek, which are called Bible languages."

"Most of the teachers in the cults deny that Jesus is the eternal Son of God, who left heaven and became a man in order to pay for man's sins by dying on the cross. They teach that **Jesus is "a" son of God** but deny that **Jesus is "the" incarnate Son of God**."(+)

"Their teaching is that Bible Christians make God cruel and uncaring when we teach that the unconverted die and suffer in hell."

"That's a total falsehood," Sarah exclaimed! "That contradicts John 3:16!" ...

"Yes", interrupted Grandpa. "Our loving heavenly father loved us when we were yet sinners, and gave Jesus to suffer the pains of hell in our place in order to forgive and save us from eternal hell.(+) But let us turn our attention to other important truths cornering **forever**."

A MIND FOCUSED ON FOREVER WILL NOT BE DISTRACTED

"**If a person's mind is centered on eternal things,** he will not have any problem forgiving those that offend or hurt him.(+) He will not let the littleness of people, or the meanness of the devil, keep him from fulfilling his short work on earth so he can enjoy God's close fellowship in the millennium."

"**If a person's mind is focused on forever,** he is very unlikely to be led into temptation, or fall into sin.(+)"

If a person's mind is absorbed in THINE IS THE KINGDOM, and the great power of all mighty God, he is not very likely to turn aside to petty things that will be burned up at the Judgment Seat of Christ. He will be focused on **Forever** or eternity, and will be working to win or disciple people."

FOCUS ON FOREVER

"The model prayer, especially our lesson today on FOREVER, is designed by God in order **to get his children to focus on eternity.**"

"There are many supporting scriptures, which teach this truth also."

"Looking unto Jesus, the author and finisher of our faith is one of those scriptures isn't it Grandpa? injected Sarah.

"Yes, Sarah it is" replied Grandpa.

"Set your affection on things above, not on things on the earth" (Colossians 3:2) quoted Tim.(+)

"Yes Tim, that is very plain isn't it? I heard Dr. Clifford Clark give a very good statement that helped me to stay focused in my ministry. The statement he made is:"

> **"I am nothing,**
> **I have nothing,**
> **I can do nothing,**
> **BUT I can do all things through Christ**
> **which strengthens me"**

"That's great!" exclaimed the kids.

"When you apply that statement to our lesson on **forever**, it is even more powerful."(+)

THINE IS THE POWER

"A person convinced of the mighty power of God and his promise to give that power to anyone that is obedient, and will ask God for that enabling grace and power **will be equipped, and do great and mighty works for God**. This success will keep him close and active in God's service. **This will help him to think in the light of FOREVER."**

"Grandpa, that is what I did before I started witnessing to Eugene. **I asked God to empower me and give me wisdom,** so that I would know what to say. (+) Boy, did he help me. It was wonderful!"

"It is all because of Jesus. We can do nothing unless he enables us. We should live in the light of thanksgiving and praise to Jesus."

"We could do that Grandpa, if our minds were constantly focused on eternity," Tim, added.

FOREVER OR ETERNITY

"Sarah, the reason this is one of the most difficult, if not the hardest of all principles to incorporate into one's life is:

"**First**, a person who lives forever, or for eternity would be **in a small minority**. He would seem strange to both family and friends. **The peer pressure would be very difficult to withstand, and most would give in to their pressure.**"

> **"I am nothing,**
> **I have nothing,**
> **I can do nothing,**
> **BUT I can do all**
> **things through**
> **Christ which**
> **strengthens me"**

"**Second**, all the distractions of the world would war against one's mind. Everywhere a person looks the world is saying, now, **now**, NOW! Do it now! Live for now!"

"**Third**, we were created from the dust of the earth and nature really calls out to us. We feel so at home in our surroundings and doing human and earthly things."

"**Fourth**, we have biological needs and a real desire to please those we love. Many times the things they want us to do are exactly opposite to living for **forever**."

"I am so thrilled that God let me glorify him by winning my friend that I want to live this way the rest of my life! Grandpa, what is the answer to overcoming all these distractions?"

"FIRST, YOU NEED TO GATHER AROUND you a close group of friends that have the same desire you have. Then meet for prayer, fellowship, and soul-winning as often as you can."

"SECOND, YOU NEED A PRIVATE PLACE OF PRAYER where you go every day and **follow this model prayer.**"(+)

"THIRD, ALWAYS REMEMBER WHAT YOU DO in this life will determine how close to Jesus you will live for 1,000 years. It will also determine what kind of blessings and fellowship you will have with him."

"Jesus promised those that were faithful over a few things, **would be greatly blessed** in the millennium." (+)

"Grandpa, Tim told you about how he did his homework assignment. I would like to tell you how I did mine. Boy, was I scared"

"What did you do, Sarah?" Grandpa asked.

"She sang a special Sunday night. It was really good, Grandpa."

"It sure was," spoke up Eugene.

"Can you sing it today, Sarah?"

"Yes, yes," the boys encouraged.

"Yes, I will. It sure has pretty words. But before I sing I want to say that I have also surrendered my life to the Lord. I'm not sure if I'll become a missionary, or" she paused and seemed to show a little embarrassment, "or marry a preacher, but I am going to Bible college and learn how to give my heavenly Father more pleasure." With that announcement, Sarah began to sing in a clear, beautiful voice.

POINTS TO PONDER

❖   **Man was created in the likeness of God and IS AN ETERNAL BEING.**

❖   **He will spend eternity either in bliss with God or in the HORRORS OF HELL.**

❖   **The bliss in heaven is so indescribable, that it will take God ages upon ages to reveal it.**

❖   **The Horrors of hell are worse than any pain and suffering found on earth, and must be endured for ages and ages, FOR ALL ETERNITY.**

❖   **The bliss of heaven will never end.**

❖   **The Horrors of hell will never end.**

❖   **Jesus suffered the pains of hell in order to redeem man to the bliss of heaven.**

WHAT WILL YOU GIVE TO SAVE MAN FROM HELL TO THE BLISS OF HEAVEN?

Lesson Thirteen

AFTER THIS MANNER THEREFORE PRAY YE: Our Father which art in heaven, Hallowed be thy name. Thy kingdom come. Thy will be done in earth, as[it is in heaven. Give us this day our daily bread. And forgive us our debts, as we forgive our debtors. And lead us not into temptation, but deliver us from evil: For thine is the kingdom, and the power, and the glory, forever.
AMEN.
Matthew 6:9-13

ADDITIONAL SCRIPTURE REFERENCE:
Matthew 6:6-15
Luke 5:5-13

LESSON THIRTEEN
AMEN

"Hello, Grandpa.   What are we going to study today?"

"Well, we finished the body of the message of the model prayer last week when we studied the subject of 'Forever'".

"Eugene sure wanted to come today, so I invited him" continued Tim.

"I really enjoyed our study last week, Grandpa, I mean…" said Eugene.

"Grandpa's fine, Eugene."

"Listen kids, what do all you young people listen for at the close of church services?"

All three stated, "AMEN."

"The service isn't over until the last **amen**! The model prayer is not over until…"

All three young people joined Grandpa in saying, "AMEN."

"Before we get to today's lessons, lets review by asking a few questions."

"What did we decide the statement by Jesus, **'when you pray, say'** was? A suggestion or a command?" (+)

A rousing answer of "COMMAND", followed.

"What relationship is God to you?"

"FATHER", exclaimed Tim and Eugene.

"HE'S OUR DADDY", answered Sarah.(+)

"What illustration did we give that shows the magnitude of God?"

"The vastness of our universe", replied Tim.

"100,000 light years across the 'Milky Way' and the hugeness of Antares and Hercules," added Sarah.

"What command did God give to Israel which applies to us today?" ask Grandpa.

All three young people quoted Psalm 81:10 in unison "I am the LORD thy God, which brought thee out of the land of Egypt: open thy mouth wide, and I will fill it."

> Thy kingdom come" is like a **FLAMING ARROW POINTING TO HEAVEN AND GOD'S ETERNAL BLESSINGS**

"Wow! You kids are on the ball!" exclaimed Grandpa." "How often is a child of God commanded to pray the model prayer? "Was the next question.

"Give us this day our daily bread" was Tim and Sarah's answer.

Eugene simply said "Daily".

"What was the first item on the prayer list which Jesus commanded his followers to pray and why?"

"**Thy kingdom come**", came the answer from all three.

"That was given to motivate God's people to always look to the second coming of Jesus, and the fellowship they will have with Him for 1,000 years," answered Tim.

"Thy kingdom come" is like a **FLAMING ARROW POINTING TO HEAVEN AND GOD'S ETERNAL BLESSINGS**," added Sarah. (+)

"You kids are too sharp for your old professor, laughed a proud grandfather. If I can't stump you – we had better get to our final lesson."

The kids protested with an "a-h-h-h-h", because they were enjoying their imprompt quiz, but Grandpa started the lesson by saying, "the account of the model prayer given by Dr. Luke does not have **thine is the kingdom and the glory and power forever, AMEN**. The statements are only found in Matthew. **The word** *AMEN* **means truly, verily, so be it.** It is used two ways, **to sanction prayer and to enforce a statement.**"(+)

AMEN, AS A SUMMARY

"We will use **amen** in all its varied meanings, as we summarize each of the parts of the model prayer. Our first summary is on '**our father which art in heaven**'".

OUR FATHER WHICH ART IN HEAVEN

He is my heavenly Father and I love Him. Let me tell you a little about my heavenly Father.

My Father is the source of all divine grace and goodness.(+)
My Father's ear is open to all who call.
My Father's hand is quick to lift the fallen and downtrodden.
My Father is the lover of us all, whether red or yellow, black or white, we are precious in his sight.
My Father supplies strength for the struggling.
My Father sustains the tempted and the tried.
My Father sympathizes with the wounded and the broken.
My Father strengthens the weak and the weary.
My Father guards the steps of the young and the old and my Father guides the wanderer home.
My Father comforts the captive and gives him fresh hope to fight on.
My Father binds up the broken hearted and gives him a new song.
*My Father is the sum total of all grace and kindness and I love him, **I love him**, I LOVE HIM.*

"These words are from the lips of one of God's greatest preachers" grandpa said, as he finished reading. All I can add is AMEN OR SO BE IT!

HALLOW BE THY NAME

Anyone as precious as my Father should be approached in humble faith and obedience. (+) He is more than my Father. The prophet Isaiah quote God in

> When Paul told his disciples **to pray without ceasing** he must have meant to talk to him as a friend

Isaiah. 57:15;

*"For thus sayeth the High and Holy One that inhabiteth eternity, whose name is Holy. I dwell in the high and holy place, with him also that is of a **contrite and humble spirit, to revive the heart of the contrite ones.**"*

"This teaches that we need to go humbly before our great Father who resisteth the proud, but gives grace to the humble. Oh, how all of us need to go along into his presence; for grace, fellowship and help in time of need. But, in addition to that, we need to walk and talk together in our daily lives as friends."(+)

"He is my friend," affirmed Sarah.

"When Paul told his disciples **to pray without ceasing** he must have meant to talk to him as a friend", commented Tim.

Grandpa states, "My friend goes with me wherever I go and I talk to him about everything. Many times I do not say 'Dear Heavenly Father,' I just start talking to him as I drive down the road. David stated he talked to his friend while he lay on his bed, **Amen.** When I walk, I talk to my friend. Hallowed be thy holy and beautiful name. The name, which is above every name. I do not mean that **we should not have a set time each day to pray,** because we must take time to enter into our closet and pray. We need to read God's Word and pray, but remember, God is always anxious to hear from and help his children. **Amen or so let it be.**"

THY KINGDOM COME

"Thy kingdom come is new to so many. They look at it as if it were a new doctrine. **It is not new, just forgotten. It is not new, it is just not practiced.**"(+)

"The Great Awakening of 1734 was led by two Methodist preachers among many others."

"John Wesley, a tireless seeker after souls, that believed that a saved person could so sin as to lose his salvation and go to hell."

"George Whitefield, a staunch Calvinist, believed in eternal salvation. George Whitefield was reputed to be a homely man that often preached with tears. His favorite and most used expression was 'Ye must be born again.'"

"It has been a mystery to me how these two men so opposite in their theological views, could work in

> The sinners in Zion are afraid; fearfulness hath surprised the hypocrites. Who among us shall dwell with the devouring fire? who among us shall dwell with everlasting burnings?
> -Isaiah 33:14

227

such close harmony and fellowship as they sought after souls. In my studies I have come to BELIEVE IT WAS THEIR COMMON VIEW OF THE MODEL PRAYER. Even to this day, 250 years after the world changing revival, some of the old time, fundamental Methodist churches are still winning souls. These soul-winning Methodist churches still begin every service by praying in unison the model prayer. They pray, 'OUR FATHER, WHICH ART IN HEAVEN, HALLOW BE THY NAME, THY KINGDOM COME." "and on to the amen."

His command to his church was, as my Father hath sent me, **EVEN SO SEND I YOU**—to save sinners.

"Jesus, commanded the apostles to pray this way. "THY KINGDOM COME."

"The great revivalists of 250 years ago, taught their members to pray—"THY KINGDOM COME".(+)

"In our day of dying churches and powerless preachers, we need to look back to the model prayer for our motivation and direction, and then pray—THY KINGDOM COME.(+) - AMEN—SO BE IT."

THY WILL BE DONE IN EARTH AS IT IS IN HEAVEN

"Heaven was so moved to save sinners from hell that it gave their Prince to make it possible."(+)

"Their Prince and our coming King, was so compassionate in his daily life that He became known as **'The friend of sinners.'** Everywhere he went, whether among Jew or Gentile, his love and message was the same. God loves you and wants to save sinners. He gave his Gospel and preached with tears. He was thought by some TO BE JEREMIAH, THE WEEPING PROPHET, BECAUSE OF HIS TEARS, which showed the compassion of God for lost souls."

"His statement for coming into the world was to 'seek and to save sinners.'"

"His command to his church was, as my Father hath sent me, **EVEN SO SEND I YOU**—to save sinners."(+)

"This prayer does deal with the future will of God for this earth in the millennium, but our job today is plain—Thy will—His will.(+) The will we should be most concerned about is to save **sinners**."

AMEN—HALLELUJAH—SO BE IT.

FORGIVE US OUR DEBTS (SINS) AS WE FORGIVE OUR DEBTORS.

"In the light of the condition which God forgives his children's sins…"

"Eugene, get this point," urged Tim "God only forgives his children's sins as **they forgive those who have wronged or sinned against them**. Excuse me; Grandpa please continue..."

"All the future blessings and glory of our earthly life depends on us having a forgiving spirit. Where you will live, the closeness and relationship you have with King Jesus depends on you having a forgiving spirit. In order to get your prayers answered you must have a forgiving spirit.. - AMEN, SO BE IT."

LEAD US NOT INTO TEMPTATION BUT DELIVER US FROM EVIL

"Man's arrogance gets him into more trouble, and destroys more lives that almost any other sin that I know."

> **What do these have in common?**
> "Give and it shall be given unto you"
> "Be ye steadfast, unmovable, always abounding in the work of the Lord"
> "WHEN YE PRAY SAY"
>
> **They are all commandments of God!**

"Man thinks he can handle it. He can, but it will **burn him.** He can handle it, but it will **scar him.**"

"He can handle it, but he will have to **live with it's consequences** throughout the rest of his earthly life and on through the millennium."(+)

King David, as a kid always did right
King David, as a servant always honored and esteemed his king
King David, as a leader always cared for his men.

"David, a king with great courage and brilliance, finally did what God had commanded him to do that other men didn't—**He drove out Israel's enemies.**"

"He loved God. He praised God. He was almost a man with **a perfect record until HE FELT HE COULD HANDLE IT**. A one-night stand turned into **a lifetime of scandal** and a history full of reproach.(+) The names of David and Bathsheba should be on a flag flown above every church, warning people **that they can not handle temptation. The only way one can handle it is to flee from it**. Obey God's command and pray every day, **Lead us not into temptation, but deliver us from evil**. - AMEN—SO BE IT."

THINE IS THE KINGDOM

"Kids, on our remaining subjects lets hear from you. We don't have much time left but... Does anyone have a question or statement concerning, '**Thine is the kingdom?**'"

Eugene raised his hand and Grandpa acknowledged by saying, "Eugene."

"Thy kingdom must be very important for it to be recognized **two different times** in this very short prayer."(+)

"It has 66 words," enlightened Sarah.

"What?" asked Eugene.

Tim spoke up, "You said this very short prayer, and Sarah gave you the number of words in the short prayer."

"Oh, thank you," responded Eugene.

"Good observation, Eugene," answered Grandpa." The difference between the usage is; **Thy kingdom come** is referring to the soon coming of the 1,000 year millennial reign of Christ on this earth. While the expression **Thine is the kingdom,** is more to emphasize God's power and ownership over this earth and universe."

"It is thrilling to think that you three teenagers living in this generation, will see God display **his mighty power over the evil rulers of this earth.**"

"He will send Jesus to smash them!" announced Sarah as she clapped her hands together for emphasis.

"Who is preaching now?" joked Tim.

"But Tim, every night we hear of the heartless terrorists and their bombing and killing innocent women and children. I can hardly wait for Jesus to come back as King of Kings and Lord of Lords and show them who is boss! **He will establish a reign of peace where love will reign instead of the hate and malice of men.**"

"You got my **amen** there!" announced Eugene.

"Amen from me or so be it," seconded Tim

THINE IS...THE POWER

"This power that he is referring to is his enabling power, which comes from being filled with the Holy Spirit."(+)

"He is not talking about tongues, Eugene," interrupted Tim.

"Jesus told the apostles that upon this rock, referring to himself as the **rock of ages, he would build his church.** Jesus builds his church **by empowering his workers with his enabling power.** He convicts the sinner, and draws the sinner toward Christ. When the sinner repents and receives Christ as his Savior, the Lord quickens him

> It is thrilling to think that you three teenagers living in this generation, will see God display **his mighty power over the evil rulers of this earth."**

with his Spirit and he is born into God's family of believers."

"God's Word is sharp and powerful and God promises that His Word would not return unto him void. Otherwise, it will accomplish the purpose for which God intended. **When a person empties himself of self and yields himself to be used by the Holy Spirit in witnessing; then God can do great and mighty things through a spirit filled man or woman.** But in our day and age, young people, there are not many people that are reminding God—**THINE IS THE POWER.** Give me thy power so I can accomplish thy work and bring you much pleasure."

"Amen," whispered Sarah.

"A big AMEN goes right there," stated Tim. "SO BE IT"

THINE IS...THE GLORY

"Young people, we are rapidly coming to a close of our studies on **the model prayer**. In this recap about **thine is the glory**, I would like for each of you to give a fact or a principle that really shows God's power and glorifies him."

Sarah's hand shot up.

"Yes, Sarah."

"Grandpa, I am constantly impressed about God making us in his image and likeness, and allowing us to live in this magnificent body. It is a vast understatement to quote, 'We are fearfully and wonderfully made.'"

> I would like to praise the Lord and give him glory **for beautifying his Saints**. I just learned that through the process of justifying his saints, that God robed every saint in the perfect righteousness of his Son.

"We praise the Lord for the awesome fleshly houses God has prepared for us."

Eugene speaks to offer his praise to God.
"How about this vast world in which we live? I have been memorizing Psalm 19: 1-4."

The heavens declare the glory of God; and the firmament sheweth his handiwork. Day unto day uttereth speech, and night unto night sheweth knowledge. There is to speech not language, where their voice is not heard. Their line is gone out through all the earth, and their words to the end of the world. In them hath he set a tabernacle for the sun.

After finishing his praise there were several amens and Tim patted his new convert on the back for his quotes and comments.

"Grandpa, I would like to praise the Lord and give him glory **for beautifying his Saints**. I just learned that through the process of justifying his saints, that God robed every saint in the perfect righteousness of his Son. (+) He does not see us as sinners but as children who are dressed in perfect righteousness. God has made us beautiful in his sight. **Praise the Lord.**"

"Let me add a couple of my own praises, young people. Let me quote the Psalmist again. "Blessed be the Lord, **who daily loadeth us with benefits**, even the God of our salvation." Psalm 68:19."

"You have heard the old song, *Count your blessings, name them one by one. Count your blessings and you will see what God hath done.* He loads or piles on so many blessings in your Grandmas and my life every day. Sitting right here before me are three of the greatest."

Different words of endearment were spoken and then Grandpa states, "the last great praise to go with these that have been mentioned is that we have God's promise that **WE CAN all graduate from life as champions or victors.**"

"In Psalm 68:23 he states, 'That thy foot (the foot of a victor) may be dipped in the blood of thine enemies.' Picturing a victorious victor, note he said, 'may be dipped,' or have victory over your enemies. That is something God offers, and **he has given**

provision of grace to accomplish it, but one must be obedient to God if he is to enjoy the victor's life."

"Kids, I am proud of you. Let go over that list of praises once again."

"We praise the Lord **for our bodies**, for we are fearfully and wonderfully made."(+)

"We praise him for **our habitat**. We live in a world that declares his wonderful glory."

"We praise him for our **eternal spiritual facelift**. God has beautified us by dressing us in the perfect righteousness of his Son. Praise the Lord, **God loads us up with so many daily benefits**. We have his promise of overcoming all enemies and **finishing life as victors**."(+)

"What a mighty God we serve!"

Amens and Praise the Lord, was followed by. - THINE IS…THE GLORY."

THINE IS…FOREVER OR ETERNAL

"Kids, in closing this final section on **forever or eternity**, I want you to remember something which really **made an impression on your mind,** and share it with us."

Tim spoke up, "Grandpa, as you know I have been in Driver's Training for the past semester, and the thing that made me really stop and think were the films they used in driver's training. I don't know where our teacher got that one film but he showed it to the class three times. **It made a person see what speed and alcohol will do to people."**

"Was the film vivid, Tim?" asked Grandpa.

"They were very vivid," was his response.

Sarah was next to give her testimony. "Grandpa, I went with Aunt Beth to a seminar when she was quitting smoking. It is unreal what type of problems cigarettes cause. They showed pictures of people's lungs and those with lung cancer, and **I'll never forget the look on some of the people's faces** who were dying with emphysema. **It made a lasting impression on me."**

Isaiah tried to make us vividly conscious of the lost when he asked, **"Who among us shall dwell with everlasting burnings?"** Isaiah 33:14.

"Kids, the reason I have drawn your attention to those vivid experiences, is **to attempt to stress the great need to get people saved from hell."**

"In Mark, the ninth chapter, Jesus referred to the body worms of those in hell **three different times**. Visualize what type of word picture he is attempting to establish in your minds. **Worms eating away at the person in hell** who is existing in a place where **the fire is never, never, never quenched."** Mark 9:48. (+)

"A person should periodically read the story of the man who fared sumptuously every day of his life **only to die and go to hell**. Luke 16:19-31. The horrible problems and heartbreak he was having then, has become a hundred times worse as he has suffered day and night for the past 2,000 years. Today he is not only suffering the same torments there in the fires of hell **but his five brothers and other family members** are there to curse and torment him **for leading them astray**."(+)

"Revelation 14:10-11 describes the horrible pain the enemies of God will suffer as the **smoke of their torments ascends upward forever and ever**. The people in this passage were lost people who suffered such excruciating pain, that they attempted to kill themselves but couldn't."

"Isaiah tried to make us vividly conscious of the lost when he asked, "**Who among us shall dwell with everlasting burnings**?" Isaiah 33:14.

"People need to look at those sitting at the dinner table and ask, **who among us will dwell with everlasting burning?**(+) Look around your classroom and ask who among us will **dwell in everlasting burning?** Look at the people who work at your job or who live on your street and ask Who? Which one? **Everlasting burning! Forever. Forever and ever. Burning!**"

"Not only do we want to try to get some vivid, eternal pictures in your minds of the need of lost people all around us, but we want to try to plant **some happy pleasant scenes of Forever in your minds as well.** The point is to try to get you TO THINK LIKE THE ETERNAL CREATURES THAT YOU ARE."

"There is a song that our generation sang when I was only a teenage boy. Your age, Tim. The words went something like this."

We are young but once and we soon, grow old, but time rolls on.

Friends at the gate won't have long to wait, because time rolls on.

Time so swiftly rolls on and on.
Time to swiftly rolls on and on.
Friends at the gate won't have long to wait,
cause time rolls *on.*

"Kids at my age, I'll soon be promoted and will belong to '**Forever.**'"

"May I leave one more eternal picture in your mind before closing."

"All three of you kids **have seen** *Star Trek* either on televisions or on a giant size screen."

"**Kid's you are a forever creature. You are programmed for forever.** You will soon be in forever. **SO, GO AND LIVE LIKE YOU ARE...FOREVER CREATURES.**"

"In Revelation 21:16-27, it pictures the Holy City **which is 1,500 miles long, 1,500 miles wide, and 1,500 miles high,** descending down from heaven to take its place on earth. You three kids, if you use your imagination, could visualize A GIANT SPACE SHIP SETTING down on earth. It is not a space ship; it is the headquarters of King Jesus.(+) But, if you consider it as a giant space ship, and get a mental image in your mind so that every time you see some movie or story about space travel, the image of the Holy City, **1,500 miles**

long, 1,500 miles wide, and 1,500 miles high would flash into your mind.

In that **Forever** City

There will be no tears…**Forever**.

There will be no death….**Forever**.

There will be no crying…**Forever**.

There will be no pain…**Forever**.

There will be no broken hearts…**Forever**.

There will be no wars…**Forever**.

There will be no more storms…**Forever**.

There will be God's Big Family…**Forever**.

"Kid's you are a forever creature. You are programmed for forever. You will soon be in forever. **SO, GO AND LIVE LIKE YOU ARE…FOREVER CREATURES."(+)**

"Thine is the kingdom, the power and the glory forever. Forever and ever and ever and ever."

—AMEN, SO BE IT.

POINTS TO PONDER

❖ Your stay on earth is described as a FEW DAYS AND FULL OF TROUBLE.

❖ You are designed to give God PLEASURE and bring him happiness.

❖ You were DESIGNED TO LIVE FOREVER.

❖ The purpose of the model prayer is to get you TO LIVE AND ACT LIKE FOREVER CREATURES.

❖ The last four principles of the model prayer lifts ones minds to the eternal. They are flaming arrows pointing toward eternity

<u>Books By the Author</u>

These booklets and books are presented to help the laymen in the local church. We are dedicated to aiding the Pastor in strengthening members through the New Convert Care Discipleship Program, we help new converts become happy, active parts of the church family.

Through the Layman Library Series, we present books designed to train and strengthen. Please contact the author for prices.

* Denote Discipleship materials
🌐Denotes – Study-to-learn-to-do-series
BULK PRICES AVAILABLE

THE LAYMAN LIBRARY SERIES

$1.75 each

100 * A Letter to a New Convert
102 How to Have Something in Heaven When You Get There
105 Incentives in Soul-winning
106 How to Pray So God Will Answer You
111 Points and Poems by Pearl - Pearl Cheeves
112 Foreknowledge in The Light of Soul-winning
113 Elected "To Go"
114 Predestination Promotes Soul-winning
115 The Ministry of Paul in the Light of Soul-winning
116 The Church, a Place of Protection, Love &Development

117 God's Discipleship Plan to Reach Multiplication

OTHER BOOKS BY DR. WILKINS

$9.95 - Foreknowledge, Election, & Predestination in the Light Of Soul-winning (160p)

$10.95 Essentials to Successful Soul-Winning (258p)

$6.95 Designed to Win (Soul winning Manuel) (120p)

$5.00 Harvest Time (110p)

$1.75 *From Salvation to Service (also in Spanish) (40p)

$1.75 * How to Be a Better Big Brother (40p)

$1.75 * Big Brother Bits (40p)

$1.75 * Questions Concerning Baptism (40p)

$3.95 * Four Tremendous Truths (61 p – Prison Edition)

$9.95* The Mission of The Church (198p)

$3.95 Four Transformational Truths (55p)

$3.95 Healing Words for Lonely People

$5.95 How To Raise A King (64p)

$5.95 Thy Kingdom Come (46p)

$7.95 The Truth About Hell (101 p)

$5.00 The Final Flight (50p)

$4.95 The Short Race Home (50p)

$5.00 Not Even a Nickel, Just A Penny (Testimony of Penny Wilkins)(40p)

$1.50 A Struggle to Peace (Cindy Benson) (58p)

STUDY-TO-LEARN-TO-DO SERIES

$9.95🌐*Milk of The Word - (Book One) (also in Spanish) (146p)

$6.95 🌐Healing Words for Hurting people (120p)
$9.95 🌐The Kindergarten Phase of Eternity (170p)
$9.95 🌐*The Meat of The Word (186p)
$9.95 🌐God's Cure for Our Nation (218p)
$9.95 🌐God's Brilliant Plan to Reach Fallen Man
        (232p)

Dr. James Wilkins, Director
New Testament Ministries

56 Arroyo Seco Circle
Espanola, NM 87532
505-747-6917
E-Mail penny@jameswilkins.org
leatherman_wave@yahoo.com